Travels with Charlie

Travels with Charlie

Days in the Broadcast Life of WSBT's Charlie Adams

by Charlie Adams

Charlie Adams
5:30 Evening News
WSBT/WHME

Diamond Communications, Inc.
South Bend, Indiana

Travels with Charlie
Days in the Broadcast Life of WSBT's Charlie Adams
Copyright © 1998 by Charlie Adams

10 9 8 7 6 5 4 3 2 1

Manufactured in the United States of America

Diamond Communications, Inc.
Post Office Box 88
South Bend, Indiana 46624-0088
Editorial: (219) 299-9278
Fax: (219) 299-9296
Orders Only: 1-800-480-3717
Website: www.diamondbooks.com

Library of Congress Cataloging-in-Publication Data

Adams, Charlie. 1962-
    Travels with Charlie : days in the broadcast life of WSBT's
Charlie Adams / by Charlie Adams
        p.   cm.
    ISBN 1-888698-19-5
    1. Adams, Charlie, 1962-   . 2. Sportscasters--United
States--Biography.   I. Title.
GV742.42.A33A3   1998
070.4'49796'092--dc21
[b]   98-33364
                                                        CIP

Contents

PART FOUR: Charlie's Guide to the Biz and the Hidden Gems of Michiana Sports

To my mother, Dr. Anne H. Adams,
who taught me so much about determination,
work ethic, and innovation.

SEPTEMBER
Friday
4

Pressure-Packed Friday Night–
An Introduction

The lights of Jim Andrews Field come into view as Chopper 22 soars towards the NorthWood High School Football Stadium. Holding my wristwatch up to the glow from the control panel lights, I make out that it's 8:34 PM. The deadline clock in my head starts to tick. It's going to be another crazy Friday night of getting our show on the air.

Adjusting my head set, I turn back towards Chopper 22 photographer Jason Scheuer, who is zooming in for an aerial shot of the field. He cuts his eyes at me enough to detect some concern in my face. This is the fourth and final stop of our helicopter tour on this Friday night. We'll be fine if we're able to land before halftime, get some highlights, and get right back in the air. If not, then we'll have to stay through the halftime break and get third quarter action. That will put us *way* behind and seriously jeapordize our chances of getting the show on the air. "Please let there be five minutes left in the second quarter," I say through the headsets.

At 1,500 feet, Chopper 22 pilot Brian Riley does high reconnaissance as the landing procedure begins. He spots the nearby baseball field, which is where we will land. He makes sure the landing zone is totally clear, then reduces the collective lever to start us down. "There's just thirty seconds before halftime," Brian says. The news stings me. We will get no second quarter action. I look down towards the scoreboard.

I can't make out the score at all. I'm amazed how Brian reads scoreboards from so high up in the sky. Eagles can't see as well as he can. Maintaining an angle to clear all obstacles in the landing area, Brian brings us down to within three feet of the ground. Hovering at that height briefly, he then lands the Bell Jet Ranger helicopter so softly that I could have sipped coffee without worrying about spilling it.

Unclicking our seat belts, Jason and I duck as we get out of the roaring chopper. Side by side, we move briskly towards the open gate in the baseball field. Thank goodness it's open. Sometimes schools forget to unlock their baseball fields for us and we look like laboratory rats scurrying around for a way out. Many times I have had to scale a tall fence, tumble to the other side, catch the camera as it's tossed over, and help the photographer huff and puff his way over, much to the amusement of the fans at the top row of the nearby football stadium.

"I should have done just three chopper landings tonight," I tell Jason as we weave through the hundreds of fans milling about the stands. "This is really pushing it. We've got to wait through a 20-minute halftime now."

"Let's try to get back in the Chopper by 9:15," Jason says.

"That way we can try to land in South Bend by 9:30," I calculate. "That's pushing it *real* close as far as getting the show on the air."

"Friday Night Fever" starts live at 10:08. When we do get back, we're going to be running around like water bugs trying to get everything put together.

First things first, though. Andrews Field is packed as the NorthWood fans watch their beloved Panthers face undefeated Concord. Opening my sack of plastic WSBT footballs like Santa on Christmas Eve, I stride onto the track and start heaving them into the stands. People go wacko trying to catch the little dobbers. You'd think I was throwing wads of $50 bills or Mark McGwire and Sammy Sosa home run balls. Little kids spill out of the stands and swarm all around me asking me to hand them a ball. The pied piper would be jealous of the line of kids behind me. "You have to be in the stands to be eligible to catch a ball," I tell them. That's my standard line to get the ankle biter kids back into the bleachers. I tell them it's IHSAA policy. That usually sounds serious enough to work. Catching plastic footballs is survival of the fittest. When I hurl one towards a chipper 10-year-old, a 15-year-old shoves him aside and snatches the ball with a sneer.

My bag depleted, I then take care of truly important business. As Jason works hard to get all kinds of video shots of the band's performance, I head for the pressbox to see what food they have to plow through. Finding three boxes of just-delivered pizza, I chomp down four pieces alongside Anthony Anderson of *The Elkhart Truth*.

At 9:05, halftime is still going on. I officially start to fret. I feel like running into both locker rooms and yelling, "Let's go teams! Get back on the field and start playing now!" Finally, at 9:08, Concord kicks off to start the third quarter. I work my way through the fans to stand alongside Jason on the NorthWood sideline.

"I zoomed in and saw you eating pizza through my viewfinder," Jason tells me flatly. "Did you bring me down some?"

"Uh. No. Anthony Anderson of *The Truth* ate it all. Uh. Yeah. That's what happened. Yeah."

Jason doesn't buy one bit of that tale.

"This game is the first game in our show," I tell Jason as he focuses in on NorthWoods first play of the third quarter. "We need something to happen, and happen fast." Presto! NorthWood quarterback Charlie Roeder hands off to running back Aaron Huber and he bolts 69 yards for a touchdown! There's a highlight! Aaron must have sensed the time crunch we're in. NorthWood kicks off. Concord fumbles the ball. NorthWood recovers. There's another highlight. Roeder completes a nice pass, which is definite highlight material, then hands off to Huber who darts in from 17 yards out for another score.

"LET'S GO!!" I yell to Jason as I scamper for the gate. It's 9:16. The show starts back in downtown South Bend in 52 minutes. Both of us sprint as fast as we can the entire 500 yards back to Chopper 22. Gasping for air, we weave through the parking lot and onto the baseball field. As I take large bounding strides, it dawns on me that eating four pieces of pizza and then doing a 500-yard dash is not recommended for 36-year-old men like me. I buckle myself in the helicopter. Brian straps in and begins the lift off routine. Of course, there are proper procedures a helicopter pilot adheres to before lift off. Dials to check. Buttons to click. I fight the urge to just reach over and pull up the lever to get us in the air! Instead, I finish buckling up as Brian goes to work. He turns the battery on, then the fuel boost pump. He makes sure the throttle is set and the starter button. He waits for 15% gas produce turbine speed, then turns the throttle on. He monitors the turbine output temperature to make sure it's not a hot start. Once the gas producer speed gets to 58%, Brian releases the starter button. He turns the generator on, and brings it to 100% operating RPM. We softly lift up and soar over the tree's surrounding the baseball field. Brian talks into his headset. "South Bend Approach Control, this is Chopper 22 heading to downtown heli-pad."

Within minutes we are going 120 MPH. Approach Control advises us of any air traffic. It's 9:30 and I'm starting to sweat bullets. Having gone to three other games this evening, we've got a lot of tape to edit. My heartbeat starts to race. The tingling panic of not getting everything together in time starts to creep in on me.

"Jason, you're going to have to edit the Bremen-New Prairie, Cassopolis-Galien, and River Valley-White Pigeon games. I'll take care of NorthWood-Concord." Jason nods.

Within minutes the lights of South Bend come into view. Our destination is the top of the Colfax Parking Garage downtown. It's a few blocks away from our TV station. Because of the deadline pressure, I consider asking Brian if we can just jump out and land on top of WSBT. Maybe we could call ahead and have them put some tumbling mats on the roof of the station. Maybe not.

At 9:34 we approach our landing sight. Brian always tries to land into the wind, so he does a dog leg around the parking garage and lands on the western side. Our landing area looks like a postage stamp from above. Focusing intensely, Brian takes us down. Still sporting a military-type haircut, Brian's years of experience from flying in the Army come shining through in moments like this. "Remember to exit the chopper to the front and stand by the railing until I have gone back up," Brian reminds us sternly as we unbuckle. As always, we exit carefully and wave goodbye to him as he roars back up and heads back to Riley Aviation in Sturgis, Michigan.

"LET'S GO! GO! GO!!"

Both of us sprint to my car, which was parked on top of the garage earlier in the day. I swerve down the levels of the vacated garage. At the bottom floor, Jason jumps out and opens the exit door. After he scampers back in, I floor it and get us onto Main Street just before a pack of cars gets to us. Every second counts at this point. Within one minute we pull up in front of WSBT and race across Lafayette Street into the building at 9:48.

Roaring through the front entrance I yell to everyone that we are back in the building. I then dash down the hallway lined with portraits of current CBS stars into the Sports office. I hastily grab the tape I will edit the NorthWood-Concord highlights onto and then snatch the matching script paper. I spin around and pounce like a lion into the hallway of edit suites. I swing the door open to edit booth 93 and slap the raw tape in and rewind it. As it rewinds I burst back out of the edit suite and into the WSBT newsroom. "Friday Night Fever" producer Jim Pinkerton meets me and informs me of a two-way call he just got from one of our many photographers that have been out shooting games.

"Greg Hilton just called in from Plymouth," he says. "There's tons of traffic for the Blueberry Festival. He's stuck in it. He may not get back with the Plymouth-Warsaw and the Rochester game highlights." It's not good news, but we have to adjust quickly and deal with it.

"If he does get back, have someone ready to help him edit," I say. "Let's float his tapes through the show and try to get them on, even if it's the last segment." Jim nods and gets back on the two-way to communicate with Greg. I fire back down the hallway and hurl myself into the edit booth. It's 9:52. Sixteen minutes remain until I have to be in the studio, with a suit on, ready to host the live, rip-roarin' show.

Bang. Bang. Bang. I make the edits of Concord-NorthWood with rapid fire motion. I put a shot of fans between every highlight. I scribble down the key information on the yellow script paper. In four minutes, I'm done. Taking huge strides, I speed back into the Sports office where I put the tape in the edit tape box and the script back in the right order. Tons of tapes are missing. So are their scripts. Photogs who have been to games all over northern Indiana and southwestern Michigan are editing furiously. I glance at my watch. It's 10:00 and only four of the 16 tapes we'll show are done.

The WSBT newscast begins. News anchor Cindy Ward introduces the lead story on the Notre Dame pep rally for the big Michigan game. A sense of dread overtakes me. This is not good. We are not ready. I grab my dress clothes and scoot into the bathroom. I dress faster than Butch Cassidy and the Sundance Kid when the posse was going into the Hotel to get them. To save time, I tied my tie earlier in the evening. I whip it over my head and tuck my shirt in. Zipping open my makeup kit, I slap on some pancake foundation. I thap myself with powder to take away some of the shine on my forehead. I rake my brush through my brillo hair. I look into the mirror for two seconds. "There. I look presentable."

It's 10:03.

Bam! Out the bathroom door I go and back down the edit suite hallway yelling, "WHO HAS A PLAY OF THE NIGHT?!" Photographer Gary Demski emerges from a booth. "I've got a good one," he says. "Mitch Thornton had an 88-yard kickoff return for Mishawaka against Adams. Do you want me to cut it?" I start to say yes when Mike Stack sticks his head out of an edit booth. "I've already cut one," he says. "Big-time kickoff return in the Lakeshore-Niles game." Boop. His head pops back in his booth. "That will work," I say. Agreeing, Gary signals me into his booth and hands me scripts of the games he has cut. "To give you an idea of what you'll have in the Notre Dame tape," he says, "I laid 15 seconds of soccer, then a shot of Pat Garrity at the volleyball game, then 15 seconds of volleyball, then pad." I thank Gary and cruise back down the hallway checking on everybody. Matt Burridge shows up from the satellite truck outside where he was editing games he shot. "Who knows how to pronounce Jason Cencelewski's name?" Matt asks about Penn's new starting quarterback. Mike Stack has a quick answer. "I'm Polish. It should be Cen-suh-less-kee." Matt nods, and scribbles down the phonetic pronunciation on his script paper.

That's our high tech way of doing things.

It's 10:05. Less than half of the tapes have been put together. Three minutes until airtime. Back in Sports, I glance over what scripts have been put in the pile. I will not have viewed hardly any of the games once the show starts. As I try to get familiar with the scribbling on the scripts, photographer A.J. Ennis pops in with the Fairfield-Churubusco script. I scan it quickly. "A.J., you've got all Churubusco plays. They're not the local team. Fairfield is. Go back and add a Fairfield play at the end." He nods and runs back to the booth. I run back into the main editing room. "Have you cut Cubs?" I ask editor Tony Fuller. "Yes. Sosa went deep. Here's the script." I grab it and put it in the pile in Sports. I then race to the front lobby where Scott Kucela is manning the phones to gather scores. "I need finals for the NorthWood, Washington, LaSalle, and Bremen games, Scott." He gives me what he has and I race back into the Sports office. A glance at the TV shows Rick Mecklenburg finishing up his weathercast. Our show is about 90 seconds away.

"WE'RE STILL MISSING FIVE TAPES!" I yell as Jim Pinkerton sorts what we do have and starts to run upstairs with them. "Jason is still cutting New Prairie-Bremen," Jim updates me. "Jim Skwarcan is doing Wawasee-Northridge." Those photogs will have to sprint upstairs with their tapes as soon as they're done. "Bring out their scripts during the show," I say as I throw on my suit jacket. Bounding down the hallway I burst through the doubledoors into the studio. Cindy tosses to the commercial break. We are 60 seconds away.

Kneeling down at my spot in the studio, I furiously organize my out-of-whack scripts for the first segment of the show, which is on Indiana games. I'll deal with the second segment at the first break. "Make sure the director knows we are floating the Plymouth and Rochester games!" I tell floor director Bob Greene as he wheels the studio camera in front of me.

Thirty seconds until airtime.

"I will do the NorthWood game off the top. The Northridge game goes from fourth to second in the rundown. After Northridge, come to me and I will ad lib about the Plymouth situation. Just roll with me." Director Bill Iddings listens intently from master control upstairs.

Twenty seconds. I still don't have my microphone on. I readjust the scripts and reach for the microphone chord. I clip it onto my tie and connect the IFB to the bottom so that I can hear the director talk into my ear piece. The little sucker won't go down the back of my shirt. It clogs up. My arms look like a backward preying mantis as I shove the chord down my shirt. Three seconds before the show, it works its way through.

The show opener starts. I take a deep breath. The red light on the camera signals we are live. Thousands and thousands are sitting at home ready to see how their community team did. "Good evening everybody. Welcome to 'Friday Night Fever'!"

"Charlie, Greg Hilton is in the building," producer Jim Pinkerton says through my earpiece as I roar into the NorthWood highlights. "Jason is going to cut his games for him." I have to listen to him as I describe the highlights. Crackling with energy, I weave through the first segment of the show. Having viewed only the game I edited, I'm totally dependent on the chicken scratch notes the photogs have written on the scripts. If I get one play out of order, then I'm like a train off the tracks.

My eyes dart from script to the monitor off to the side. Game after game is shown. I hold on like I'm riding the orneriest bull at the rodeo.

Needing a respite, I introduce Matt Burridge, who is sitting on a stool in front of our locker room set across the studio. Matt narrates the St. Joe-Goshen and Penn-Elkhart Central game highlights that he shot. As he does that, I fall to my knees to double-check that my remaining scripts are in order and to get a better feel for the games I'm about to narrate. I circle names of players and draw lines between play descriptions to avoid losing track once I'm back on. Matt finishes up and tosses it back to me. As the show rumbles on I start getting giddy. Heck, why not? It's a semi-miracle we've gotten everything on to this point. I start going "woooooooo" and "weeeeeeeee." A viewer might think I'm on some sort of muscle relaxant or something.

The first segment comes to an end and commercials start rolling. I reach over for a cup of water that Bob Greene was nice enough to get for me and gulp it like a parched wild animal. Jason bursts into the studio and hands me the scripts for the River Valley and Cassopolis games that he has just finished editing. I scan his writing. It looks like aliens wrote it. Our photogs are notorious for having handwriting that's scribblier than doctors' prescription notes.

Scott Kucela runs into the studio and peels off four different final scores, which I jot down onto the Michigan notes.

"They're still cutting the Plymouth and Rochester tapes," Jim Pinkerton says through my ear piece. "Tease them to the final break." I make a mental note and sort my scripts for segment two. I'll worry about segment three when it gets here.

The commercials end and I peel into the second segment, which focuses on Michigan. I woop and holler my way through the games. Mike Stack eases into the studio and perches himself on the locker room stool. I toss to him to narrate the Michigan games he shot that evening. The second segment ends and we go to commercial again. Jason rushes back into the studio and hands me the freshly written scripts for the Plymouth and Rochester games. "What the heck is this?" I ask Jason. The scripts say "#20 with good tackle" and "Plymouth defense does well."

"Don't we have players names?"

"We didn't have time to write them down," Jason says as the red light on the camera comes back on. I'm on live.

"Wooooo. Welcome back. Hey! We've got those Plymouth-Warsaw highlights in! Roll 'em!" Director Bill Iddings rolls the tape and I say "wooooooo" a lot since I have little to no information on my script sheet. "Look at that effort!" and "How about that!!" work as several plays are shown. The Rochester game follows and it's more of the same. "Look at that guy run!" I say as a Rochester player zips all over the field. At this point, the rollercoaster known as "Friday Night Fever" has gone through its wildest loops and now it's just a matter of riding it in. I cruise through the rest of the sports coverage, say goodnight, and the credits roll. Around me on the floor are over 40 sheets of script paper that I used. I look up at the studio lights and wonder how the heck did it all come together again. Feeling like I've been hit by several Transpo buses, I wander like a punch drunk boxer into the newsroom where everyone is polishing off the Papa John's pizzas that are delivered each Friday night. Pirannah's don't go through cows in the river any faster than our people go through pizza. Everybody stands around and shares war stories about their particular time crunch. The pizza is polished off and everyone heads their different ways. I walk slowly back into the Sports office and take off my tie, thinking about how calm it is now. Just a half hour earlier, everyone was running around like crazy. They knew exactly what they had to do. They did it. The show got on.

Barely.

No wonder I started getting gray hairs about the time I turned 30. This line of work is one adventure after another. It's unpredictable, rewarding, and extremely challenging.

In this book, I will take you *back* through a three-month stretch to show you the things I do and the people I cover. The timeframe will be mid-February to mid-May of 1998. During that period, I'll take you through one particular week in detail to show you exactly how a broadcast week unfolds.

I feel that you will learn some things, laugh a little, and have a good time. The TV News media often emphasizes negative news over positive news. The one thing I hope you take away from this book is that there are a lot of remarkable people out there whose stories or organizations should get more airtime because of how they inspire others.

—*(Chopper) Charlie Adams*

Part One
February 17-March 3, 1998

I Didn't Know You Were So Tall and a Story about John Grisham

I've been in local TV News as a sportscaster for 16 years, ever since I was a junior in college. In that time I've produced and anchored over 10,000 sportscasts. These days I'm "having my professional horizons broadened." Not long ago, WSBT General Manager/President Jim Freeman and News Director Meg Sauer talked to me about changing my role at the station.

I pictured them telling me that my new job would be to maintain station vehicles. Actually, they said they wanted me to still be "the sports guy" (BIG BOARD SPORTS!) *and* start a regular feature called "Making a Difference." The segment would run in News. It would profile the many people and organizations that make a difference in our community. I enthusiastically agreed. I love local sports and always want to be covering everything from the rich tradition of Notre Dame football to Indiana's legendary passion for high school basketball. Doing "Making a Difference" would allow me to grow professionally and bring attention to some good causes and special people. Having done over 7,000 sportscasts at WSBT over the years, I was excited about also putting together positive features in news.

On this Tuesday, February 17th, the "Making a Difference" feature I'm taping is on the Montessori Academy Educational program at the

Center for the Homeless in South Bend. Pete Webb had written the station to tell us about the program. It's for children three to six years old and plays a key role in breaking the cycle of homelessness. These homeless children are taught important things that their parents are often lacking: self-sufficiency, perserverance, respect for others and the environment, discipline, integrity, and the moral strength of self.

WSBT photographer Laurent Lecomte and I are greeted by teacher Sandy White as we arrive to tape the feature. After we move upstairs to the classroom, I stand off to the side and listen to Sandy as she enthusiastically tells me all about the program. Laurent deftly moves about the room getting video for the story. When we usually think about the homeless, we think of a grown man with a scraggly beard and a bulky dark green jacket. Actually seeing precious young homeless *children* in person startles me.

My photographer Laurent is from Saint-Vallier, France, which is south of Lyon in the Rhone Valley. After two years of Technical and Audiovisual School in France, he came to the U.S. with a scholarship to spend nine months here. WSBT News anchor Mike Collins met Laurent when Mike was overseas previewing Notre Dame's 1997 football trip to Ireland. Mike set it up where Laurent got to work at WSBT. Laurent is spirited and "peppy" all the time. When he leaves WSBT, he'll do his required military service at the Elysee Palace under French president Jacques Chirac.

As Laurent gets video, Sandy tells me permanent funding for their program is not concrete. If you or your business would like to play a vital role in the lives of homeless children, call (219) 282-8700.

As Laurent and I leave the Center for the Homeless, a fella outside on the snow covered street recognizes. "I didn't know you were so tall, Charlie," he observes. *That* is the comment I get most often when I'm out covering a story or walking in the mall or doing whatever. I'm not kidding when I say I hear that about 1,000 times a year. That's probably a conservative estimate. "You don't look that tall on the News," they'll say. "All of you News people look the same height behind that set." I generally nod and say that the newscast producers lower my anchor seat which makes my legs look like a preying mantis as they try to fit under the set.

"Just how tall are you anyway?" they'll ask.

"I'm 6'5" or so," I'll respond.

"How tall are the other anchor people?" they'll query.

"Well, veteran News anchor Luke Choate is a legal pygmy actually. He's got stumpy legs. Can't be over four and a half feet tall. What makes him look taller is his poofy anchor hair. The floor director and studio camera crew prop him up on two Indianapolis phone books just before he anchors the news. Sometimes he'll lose his balance and fall off. Co-Anchor Debra Daniel will be reading a news story and you'll hear Luke go 'wooompf.' It's sort of a muffled sound with a trace of Luke going, 'arrgh!' He's like a weeble that wobbles the wrong way. A lot of of loyal, daily viewers will turn to one another on their couch at home and say, 'little Luke just fell out of his anchor seat.' The floor director has to hastily put him back in his anchor seat and poof up his hair before Debra finishes her news story."

I don't actually say all that, but am tempted to spin such a tale.

Over the years I've had so many people say "I didn't realize you were so tall" that I've thought about putting a height chart right by me on BIG BOARD SPORTS. The six-foot mark would be around my neck and viewers at home could go, "Look. He's tall. About 6'5."

The "how tall are you?" doesn't really bug me. Another thing that comes in droves is "the call." Of all the phone calls I get in the WSBT Sports office, the most frequent question is: "What day is the Super Bowl and when does it start?" I start getting these calls in the Fall. Usually it's nice ladies that don't follow the NFL that much, but are planning their Super Bowl parties. I always make sure to have the date and time written down near my phone.

With it being February, it's the heart of basketball season. After taping the feature at the Center for the Homeless, I put my "sports hat" on, so to speak, and head to Notre Dame to report the 5 o'clock Sports segment live at the Joyce Center. The Irish are hosting national power UConn. Notre Dame coach John MacLeod is always gracious enough to join me live courtside at 5:22 PM to talk about Irish home games. Since John is such a sharp dresser, I always wear my spiffy suit to try to be near his *G.Q.* level. Nice clothes just flow on the classy MacLeod. Same with Pat Riley. Me? They just frump on me. For starters, I've got a dip in my shoulder so the tailor has to put foam padding in one shoulder of all my coats. That makes me look like half Bulkoid Man. Speaking of clothes, an Elkhart clothing store used to bring the male anchors at WSBT News suits each week. For a few years there we were looking slick. My general routine would be to wear comfortable clothes into work and then about 10 minutes before the 5:20 TV News sportscast, I'd run into the anchor clothes closet and put on my new suit of the day. That was usually fine, except sometimes the store folks would accidentally put Luke's dress pants in with my stuff. I would put one of my long legs in and go, "oh oh." First, I had to wedge my leg back out. Then I'd desperately yank another pair of pants off the rack and hope they'd go with the tie that was already tied.

Despite my fashion adventures, I love days like this one. Bigtime Big East Conference basketball in South Bend. I usually sit in the second press row near the court. I'm assigned the seat right behind whoever is in town to do the play-by-play and color commentary for whatever network the game is on. That means, since the press rows aren't elevated, I'm looking right into the back of their heads. Over the years I have stared at many different toupee styles. I've marveled at how real some are and usually spend TV timeouts trying to detect where the mesh is of real hair and toupee hair.

The Winter Olympics are underway on CBS, which is our network affiliate. We have Notre Dame hockey coach Dave Poulin come into the WSBT studio for a live on-set appearance on the 11:00 newscast. Dave is going to be our expert analyst for the Olympic hockey games—something he did for a Boston station while he was with the Bruins in the NHL. He is an *extremely* sharp man who has a dynamic presence during all of the on-set appearances for us.

Dave gets to the station a little early and we chat back in the sports office (which is about the size of a NHL penalty box). He asks if I have read the latest John Grisham book called *The Street Lawyer*. He says it sends a strong message about giving to the poor and the homeless. I tell Dave my wife Sherrad has her clamps on the book but that I'm going to read it as soon as she is done because I am a big Grisham fan.

Author JOHN GRISHAM

My wife Sherrad and I are probably his biggest ambassadors in South Bend.

Here's the deal on that. When I left WDSU-TV in New Orleans in 1992, we moved up to my hometown of Oxford, Mississippi. I took a job with a local radio station and basically took about a year off from the TV News business. Despite winning the Associated Press Award for Best Sportscast in New Orleans and all of Louisiana, the experience I had at the TV station in New Orleans was a doozy (three different news directors in the first few months) so I wanted to step back for a while.

Grisham lived just outside of Oxford where he and his family had a beautiful home on a hill. You could see it from the road that leads into Oxford.

Grisham has always loved the sport of baseball, so he had a baseball field built on his property for local Little Leaguers to play. It even had a Fenway Park Green Monster wall in the outfield.

Grisham was red hot with *The Firm and The Pelican Brief* having sold 18 trillion copies. He was being pulled every direction by the success of his career, but he had a reputation for always taking the time to respond to letters from fans and was known as a true southern gentleman. Oxford, with a population of about 20,000, had been home to reknowned author William Faulkner, so the townfolk were somewhat used to an internationally known author and pretty much let him go about his business without hanging all over him in the Post Office line.

At the time, I was doing a lot of local radio work including play-by-play of the University of Mississippi women's basketball team. I learned that their coach, Van Chancellor, had coached Grisham in grade school in Grisham's hometown of Southhaven, Mississippi. I put a call into Grisham's office and within a day or two got a call back from Grisham. I wanted to write a story on their relationship for "The Ole Miss Spirit." I was a freelance writer for the weekly paper that covered University of Mississippi athletics.

Grisham talked with me for 15 minutes about his junior high days when he played basketball. Chancellor and his wife Betty lived in a trailor home 50 feet from the gym. Grisham and his buddies used to show up at 7:30 in the morning at the trailor to get the gym keys. Sundays after church, the Chancellors would be eating lunch when Betty would see Grisham's head pop up in the window like he was on a pogo stick. He was looking in to see if he could get the gym keys again.

Grisham called himself a pretty bad player. Chancellor diplomatically said that Grisham's "wit was quicker than his feet."

I have enjoyed reading Grisham's books. I admire him because he doesn't use offensive language and still gets his point across. I like the fact he's put the Hollywood fat cats in their place when dealing with the movie rights to his books. He has fired zingers at law firms that work their people to death and obviously don't care about workers having balance in their lives. He has womped the big, bad insurance companies and in his latest book delivers a strong message about the poor (I have to take my wife's word on that because she bought the book the first day it came out and hasn't let me get my hands on it yet).

FEBRUARY
Wednesday
18

Farewell to Harry

Assignment Editor John Snyder calls our house pretty early. Big John is the hub of the WSBT-TV newsroom. His job is to coordinate the coverage of all the stories that end up on the newscasts. A Penn High and Bethel College grad, John is an extremely intelligent and gentle man who gained tremendous respect some years ago with his daily news coverage as a reporter in southwestern Michigan. From there he started doing Charles Kuralt-quality features for the news. John would often travel with me on Notre Dame football trips. I would do stories of the Fightin' Irish getting ready for the game. John would do special features on the fans and the community the game was being played in. In 1994, when Notre Dame was in Orlando to play Florida State, John and I were racing against the clock to get several stories shot and edited. We were hastily leaving the Orlando Chamber of Commerce (John was doing a story on the city) when we zipped through a drive-through to get a bite to eat. Knowing we had to be at a local TV station in 10 minutes to edit, John hit the accelerator hard coming out of the drive-through and all our food spilled on the floorboard of the car. Hungry, and with no time to reorder, we picked french fries off the floor and gobbled them down the whole time as we drove to the station.

Besides being a veteran TV newsman, John is in his second year as fire chief at Penn North Fire Department. He oversees a department that has about 25 volunteers, two stations, eight pieces of equipment, and about a $200,000 budget. They respond to about 700 incidents a year and cover about 28 square miles. John became a fire station volunteer as soon as he was old enough (18). He loves it! He even collects fire memorabilia at home, and owns a 1939 American-LaFrance firetruck, which he's restoring at a snail's pace. His organizational skills led WSBT to ask him to take over the mammoth and extremely important job of assignment editor in the newsroom. Personally, I'd rather see John doing features in the field. I think he's right up there with Kuralt.

On this particular morning, Big John is calling our house early because Executive Producer Tim Ceravolo has decided to send sports reporter Mike Stack, photographer Jason Scheuer and the WSBT satellite truck to Chicago. It's the bottom of the ninth with two outs, two strikes, and nobody on base in broadcaster Harry Caray's life. He has been very sick for the past week. At first I resist their decision to send our crew to Chicago and my feelings have nothing to do with the magnitude of the story.

On the phone, I tell John that the Midwest Regional video feed we take at the station will have all sorts of coverage on Harry, including reaction from fans in Chicago and Cubs out in Arizona. My problem is that sending Mike leaves just me back here with a lot of local sports on tap. It's Matt's day off and as a boss, I am a big believer in my reporters getting their two days off as regularly as possible. If people don't have balance in their lives and steady time off, it's hello burnout. Executive Producer Tim assures me that the three local games will be covered that night, so that makes me feel better. The sandy haired, athletically built Tim is a recent addition to the WSBT newsroom. He's come from WTHR-TV where he was an award-winning executive producer and planning editor in the impressive and high tech Indianapolis market, so he has a lot of great ideas and a "get it done" intensity that is good for any newsroom. I like that he emphasizes that all kinds of news get covered and that a newscast is not 80% "negative" news. He's good at what he does. Real good.

When I get to work, I put together a feature on Jimtown High School twin basketball players who are incredible in the classroom. Andy Namanye has made straight A+'s with a few A's sprinkled in all four years of high school! It's one of the highest grade-point averages (4.18) in the history of Jimtown (which has wonderful community support and young people). In the story Andy tells WSBT, "Our parents never pushed us to be the best, but to do the best we can." His twin brother James is ninth academically in the senior class. James will go to IU for their Medical School. As a high school senior, he is in the co-op program at Elkhart General Hospital where he works in the E.R. "It helps me see if I really want to be a doctor or not," says James. He says since the boys were in third grade their parents insisted homework be done before they could go outside and play.

We've had the opportunity to do stories on some outstanding young people over the years, primarily in the Burger King WSBT High School Athlete of the Week segment. It airs Thursday's on the 6:00 News. Pete Gaff of New Prairie High School ranks among the all-time best that we have featured. A baseball and basketball standout, Pete scored a 1490 on the SAT. He won academic-oriented contests in French and Speech. He's in the capella choir and spends a lot of time helping his church reach out to the poor, hungry, and homeless. His mother, Becky, told the *South Bend Tribune* how Pete avoided the teen perils of drugs, alcohol, and teen sex. "His time was occupied," Becky told the *Tribune*. "He had no time for those pursuits. We had him set goals in the seventh grade. He wanted to be as good as he could be."

The WSBT All-Star charity basketball team is in action tonight at Grissom Middle School. Angela Overmyer, a teacher at Grissom, arranged the game to help raise money for the eighth graders' trip to Washington, D.C. An overflow crowd comes for the game which is a strong positive statement to the kind of school Grissom is and the support the parents give the students. Shannon Carter of Sunny 101.5 FM hits some jump shots early for us, but the Grissom faculty take us apart. Former Bethel College star Mark Galloway, as luck would have it, is now a teacher at Grissom and he dunks three times on us. Bethel assistant coach Scott Laplace, who is "Mr. Grissom," plays all right for an old guy. Our team has such WSBT notables as myself, Norm Stangland, Paul Kiska, Ed "pasty white legs" Ernstes, Jonathan Miller, Bob Montgomery of "J.T. in the Morning," and the bearded weather wonder, Bob Werner. Among those in attendance is the realty dynamo Joel Roth. I'm always telling Joel that I want to speak at the Builders Association Convention so I can get them to start building doorways higher. I'm tired of always ducking. If people think I'm tall, wait until they see what's coming. Heck, there's an eighth grader at Dickinson Middle School who is 6'7"!

The benefit game ends up raising about $1,500. The WSBT All-Stars are always glad to help area schools or charities raise money. The team has a rich tradition. WSBT's Rick Carter tells me that once Joe Montana played for the All-Stars. I'll bet that was a thrill for Joe that ranks right up there with his late TD pass to beat the Bengals in the Super Bowl.

Mike Stack's coverage from Chicago is very professional. Mike is a lifelong Cubs fan and that comes across as this story has deeply saddened him. Harry passes away in the early evening. Mike gets touching reaction from folks at Harry's Restaurant and does a live segment off the top of the 11PM News outside Wrigley Field. Photographer Jason shows a live shot of fans gathered outside Wrigley remembering the one and only Harry.

Being a lifelong fan of the game of baseball, veteran news anchor Mike Collins crafts a touching tribute to Harry's contributions to the game. Not only is Mike one of the premier writers in all of TV News, he also knows exactly how to read the copy. His voice inflections, pauses, and clarity reflect his years of experience and intelligence. Mike spends most of the evening in an extremely focused state putting this all together. It certainly shows as it airs during the 11:00 newscast.

Mike Stack has been a very valuable part of the WSBT Sports staff and the station in general. The 30-year-old Stack is from South Bend. He played baseball at LaSalle High and went on to graduate in Communications from IU. The Hoosiers won the '87 National Championship when Mike was in Bloomington. Since Mike has followed the Cubs since he was a young 'un, I asked him to give his memories of Harry and reflect on his coverage during this solemn time in Chicago and all of Cubsdom:

I became a Cubs fan in 1974 when my parents got cable TV. I remember watching my very first game on WGN as Steve Stone and Steve Swisher made up the battery. I had always hoped that someday my job would take me to Wrigley Field. On Wednes-

day, February 18, 1998, it did. But, sad to say, I wish I did not have to go for the reason which I did. Harry Caray had been in a coma for three days and the outlook was not good. Photographer Jason Scheuer and I made the drive to the Windy City. I've made the trip to Wrigley maybe 50 times. $1.55 toll at Portage, .50 before the Skyway, two bucks back off the Skyway, Stoney Island to Lakeshore Drive to the Belmont Exit to Clark Street, nine blocks north—voila! Wrigley Field (I still get chills those last nine blocks!).

Jason is a brilliant photographer who is a master innovator. It's never the usual with Jason. And I got the feeling, by his work, that he realized how important, as a Cub fan, this was to me. I actually didn't realize how important this was to me until we got to Gary. As a kid, getting to Gary meant you were at Chicago's front porch. That's when the goose bumps start. On our trip in February, I remember looking out an an old building that had been restored. I think it's called the American Bridge Company. As I looked at that building, I remembered my dad telling me the structure was there when he was a little boy travelling to Chicago (probably not to a Cub game. He's a Dodger fan—God help him).

At that point, all the trips I made with my family and friends going to Cubs games hit me. For me as a reporter, when I have to do stories that include "live" shots, I get kind of anxious. I wouldn't call it nervousness. I just want to be as prepared as I can be so that things will run flawlessly. I thought to myself, "You've been a die-hard Cubs fan since you were six years old. Let's do this up right. This guy has brought so much joy to your years of growing up. This one's for Harry!"

In spite of having to work, really work against the clock and deadlines, there was no anxiety or worries. I just went with the flow. And it went so smoothly, probably because I am a Cub fan. I felt what the fans felt. For the "live" shots, there wasn't a whole lot of rehearsing because the lead-ins to my stories were simply from the heart. I was just saying, in so many words, what any Cub fan would say: "Harry, we love you. We'll miss you. But as long as there are ivy-covered walls at Clark and Addison, you will always be."

We wound up staying until Thursday evening. We did seven stories and six "live" shots in two days. The following week we went back to Chicago for Harry's funeral. Two more stories and two more "live" shots. We hustled like Shawon Dunston stretching a single into a triple and were safe at third—we got the job done. But you know what? I'll never forget what Jason said to me when we were finally finished. "It didn't even seem like work."

It never does when you love what you're doing.

FEBRUARY
Friday
21

How People Move around in TV News

When I come into the WSBT today, meteorologist Sam Scaman bounces into the Sports office. "You've probably heard," Sams says excitedly. "I'm going to Minneapolis!" I had heard the rumors the past few days, but my new policy of *trying* not to participate in newsroom gossip has kept me from asking Sam if it were true. That's great news. Sam has worked very hard since 1989 for WSBT. He has a tremendous passion for weather and puts forth a great effort every day. The station in Minneapolis has recognized his on-air ability, his enthusiasm, his knowledge of weather and of all the computer graphics involved. Sam's knowledge of weather computers is extraordinary. When looking for a meteorologist, many stations don't appreciate that when they look at video resume tapes. Minneapolis was smart enough to realize Sam knew his trade inside and out.

While most folks would aspire to work in warm weather climates like Phoenix, Atlanta, or San Diego, Sam's top choice was Minneapolis because of the challenge of forecasting the snow there. One time I was talking with Sam's wife Liz and she jokingly lamented that wherever they moved in the future it would be someplace "with a lot of snow."

I asked Sam to give us a "blow by blow" account of how he ended up with the Minneapolis job. This should give you some insight as to how folks move around in this profession:

I received a call from the news director at KMSP-TV (Minneapolis) in late November. He said he had seen my work and wanted to know if I was interested in coming up and interviewing for their chief meteorologist position. After 45 minutes of talking on the phone, we agreed on a weekend visit in December.

After the tickets were purchased and arrangements were made, it was discovered that my wife needed surgery on her gums and our two-and-a-half-year old son Patrick needed his tonsils out. He had developed sleep apnea and a horrible snoring problem. Their surgeries were within a few days of each other and a few days before my interview in Minneapolis. Thank goodness, the surgeries went well and so did the interview.

At the time, I was in the middle of new contract negotiations with WSBT. After almost nine years at the station, we agreed to a new three-year contract with a six-market 'out' clause. Meaning, that if I was offered and accepted a chief meteorologist position in any of those six cities, then my contract with WSBT could be terminated. Keep in mind, I loved WSBT and all of the people there. I just didn't want to leave to go anywhere. I had been offered jobs before, but the situations were not better than WSBT. WSBT had provided me with the most advanced weather computer systems in the world. Why would I want to leave all of that technology for less—even though the market size was a little larger? It was going to take a lot ot take me away from such a wonderful place.

In January, I got the call. KMSP in Minneapolis had offered me the job. It was now time for us as a family to seriously discuss the opportunity and make a decision that would change our lives forever. The number of television viewers in a market determines the size of that TV market. I was looking at moving from market 85 (South Bend) to market 14. They were offering a substantial salary increase. That was an important factor, but not the most important in deciding to move my family.

The two most important ones that we needed to consider were:

(1) Was Minneapolis a good place to raise our children? and (2) was KMSP a place where I could be happy? After much

research, debate, talking with friends and colleagues, we discovered the answers to both of those questions were yes. In mid-January, I accepted the new position, and talked with both Jim Freeman, president and general Manager of WSBT, and News Director Meg Sauer. Jim put his arm around me and said if there is anything he could ever do for me to just ask. Meg said that I deserved the opportunity, that I have worked long and hard for it.

It was in my contract that I needed to give eight-weeks notice to WSBT. This was mainly to help the station find a replacement and take care of all the transitions that and main anchor change requires. KMSP had no problem with this arrangement. My new boss said he didn't want me to burn any bridges at WSBT. I told him not to worry, the last thing I would ever do would be to cause any problems at a place that I loved.

Since we were soon going into February ratings period, the news of my new job would be kept secret for a while. KMSP agreed as well, so everyone sat on the job announcement and remained silent. After about a month, rumors began to fly and I started getting calls. Since I didn't want to lie to any of my friends, I told them that I have never had any relationship with Monica Lewinsky. By making a reference to the presidential scandal going on at the time, I side-stepped the question and in vague way gave them the answer they were wanting to know. Within a few weeks, an official memo was released and everyone talked openly about the opportunity. We were lucky. After putting our house on the market, it sold within four days. Joel Roth was our realtor. He has to be one of the hardest working and best realtors in the South Bend area. Next, we had to find a new home in Minneapolis. KMSP took care of all of the expenses for a house hunting trip in early March. We walked through 18 homes in two days, and found what we were looking for: a pretty home, in a great neighborhood, with lots of children, in a great school district.

My last day at WSBT would truly be one of the most emotional days I've ever gone through. Jim Freeman scheduled a "going away" staff meeting in the studio. Photographer Jason Scheuer had made a 30-minute good-bye tape. It was funny and emotional with everyone at the station saying their good-byes.

After everyone watched the tape, Jim had my wife and me come to the podium. He announced to everyone not to be sad, that they will all see us again in the future. He said the reason he knew this, was because of an envelope which he held in his hand. In this envelope were tickets to a Notre Dame football game, along with roundtrip airline tickets and a weekend stay at the downtown Marriott. When Jim gave us the envelope, Liz began to cry. Then I saw tears coming from Jim's eyes. As I stepped up to the microphone, I began to cry. My stomach was in knots, my eyes were producing as much water as a cumulonimbus cloud, and I was trying to tell everyone good-bye. WOW! I told everyone that WSBT is just a building with walls. But it is the people that work within those walls that make it so special!

The next morning as we drove out of town, we cried again. South Bend had been good to us. We were truly going to miss her.

I knew it was a matter of time before a big market grabbed Sam. Still, it's hard to picture him gone because he's been such a big part of the news for almost a decade. Over the years, Sam spoke to hundreds and hundreds of elementary students about weather. He also always got to WSBT early so he could get a lot of his forecasting work done. That way he was able to spend a couple of hours at home with his family at night and help Liz put their young children to bed before coming back to do the late news weathercast.

Sam has always emphasized his faith in God and his commitment to his family. Another former WSBT employee who took a strong stand there was Sports Director Tim Swore (1991-1993, that's not how long he lived but how long he was at WSBT). Tim made it clear that his faith in God was #1 priority. Not long after Tim left WSBT in 1993 to become weekend sports anchor in Cincinnati, I was driving with a photographer to cover the NCAA Tournament in Lexington, Kentucky. The photographer looked over at me and said, "You're not going to read your Bible in the hotel room like Tim are you?"

Tim worked hard at WSBT, but his priorities were in order. God came first. After doing an outstanding job in Cincinnati, Tim was hired by a Detroit TV station to be sports director. What does that tell you? Sam Scaman and Tim Swore are two men who are raising families while being very involved in their respective churches. They are both in key positions in two of the top TV News markets in America making outstanding salaries. It shows you don't have to be a workaholic to climb up in business. They have let God take control of their lives and with Him in charge they're doing great things professionally.

I Can't Believe I Ate the Whole Paczki

For the second year in a row, I've been invited by Meijer to be in its annual Paczki Eating Contest. At 1:45 I get to the Meijer on Bremen Hwy 331 where I will shortly woof down a month's worth of fat grams in two minutes. Various celebrity folks from the community are also there as contestants.

Once the competition starts we each have two minutes to engulf as many of the round, sugar coated, fruit filled Polish pastries as possible. Six paczkis are put on each of our platters. They're filled with up to two ounces of premium jelly, traditionally prune, raspberry, lemon, or custard. To top it off, they're fried.

As if I'm going to eat six of these baseball-sized deals in 120 seconds. I'd swell up and burst, giving the station a strong lead news story on the 5:00 newscast. *"Good evening, I'm anchorman Luke Choate. Charlie Adams has imploded. Let's go live to Debra Daniel who is at the scene."* Ah, well. I'll have fun and chomp away because it's the spirit of the paczki season! This time of year it's fun to hear folks in South Bend pronounce "paczkis." You hear "pooch-key" and "punch-key" and even "poonch-key."

It's a Polish tradition to eat them the day before Ash Wednesday. At first, years ago, they were made to use up the eggs and lard that were not allowed during Lent. Nowadays, they're a last day sweet treat before the sacrifice and abstinence of Lent.

Sharply dressed store manager Rick Zeeff sits us down over in the Deli area. Customers have stopped shopping to watch us get silly. Having done this last year, I really like this whole concept. It's fun and it raises a lot of money for charity. The winner gets $2,000 to donate to his or her favorite charity. All the other contestants get about $200 (based on how many paczkis Mejier sells) to give to their favorite charity.

The competition starts and defending champ Bill Carnegie of the North Central Food Bank plows in and builds the early lead. Having heard that frequent sips of water helps the paczkis slide down, I try that strategy. Strawberry fillings and powdered frosting get all over my cheeks and nose as I take big chomps. The customers howl with laughter as we get so messy that we look like two-year-olds in a high chair at dinnertime. Carnegie whips us all, polishing off theee in two minutes. I eat about two and a half. "At a Meijer store in Detroit a man once ate four-and-a-half in two minutes," Zeeff tells us. I bet they had to carry that guy off. Must have been Cecil Fielder.

Shannon Carter of Sunny 101.5 spits out the remnants of her second paczki. She designates her charity portion be given to the American Cancer Society. I pick the Hope Rescue Mission in downtown South Bend, which has been serving the needy and the homeless since 1954. The first "Making a Difference" story I ever did was at "the Hope." They affirm the image of God to each person to make choices, to take responsibility, and to find constructive answer's to life's problems. They need financial support to meet the challenges ahead. With changes in family structures and the challenge of welfare reform, *women and children* are the fastest growing population seeking Mission services. They are preparing for that as well as many other exciting projects like a community center.

Meijer stores held seven Paczki contests this year—Detroit, Toledo, Fort Wayne, Grand Rapids, South Bend, Anderson, and Indy. Through the contests they were able to give more than $15,000 back to the communities. My mistake this year was having eaten lunch too soon before the competition. Next year I vow to show up starving. Between learning of water sipping and being in a starved mode, I just know I'll beat Carnegie next year. Meijer's Steve Van Wagoner had might as well etch my name on the 1999 trophy already!!

The highlight of the afternoon back at the station comes at 3:30 when state champion wrestlers Brad Harper of Mishawaka and Jason Carr of Wawasee arrive for our famous "tour" of the WSBT Empire. Both went 44-0 for the season which is remarkable. I lead them around the building doing all sorts of silly things for a segment that will air at 6:00. We have Brad thumb-wrestle zany Sunny 101.5 DJ Phil Brittain. In the WSBT-TV newsroom, Jason puts Luke Choate in a double leg take-down and demonstrates a half-nelson to anchor Debra Daniel.

In an edit booth, I get Jason to read something that I edit into the piece. It's jokingly meant to sound as if these were Jason's impressions of WSBT. In actuality, it's something I wrote earlier in the day: "I am so impressed with the thoroughness, resourcefulness and commitment to excellence of the news staff here," Jason *says.* "I get a warm, fuzzy feeling knowing my news viewing needs will always be met by WSBT. I also am impressed that the station routinely checks for ticks."

The "Making a Difference" feature for this week airs tonight. It's on the Special Services Department at the St. Joseph County Public Library in downtown South Bend. Nancy TenBroeck of the library says they are trying to get the word out about it. "We have a lot of services for those who are blind or visually impaired, hearing impaired or deaf, those that need English as a second language, and reading skills for adults looking to learn or improve their literacy skills." The adult literacy programs especially struck a chord with me, because while I was there taping a segment, a man was in to improve his reading skills so he could become an electrician.

People from the community can come in and learn how to teach others how to read. Pat Fogarty of WSBT Sales has been training to know how to teach others how to read. They would love to have you do that also!

Anne Raymer does a great job as head of Special Services. Susan Shank is the vital first person that an adult new learner meets when they come in. They're usually frightened or apprehensive, but Susan is marvelous at gently reassuring them and signing them up for the literacy program. The Special Services Department also has an outstanding tutoring program for elementary and middle school students as well as many more things. Call them at (219) 282-4655 for more information.

FEBRUARY
Thursday
26

A College Football Great Visits South Bend

The only two-time Heisman Trophy winner is in South Bend today. Ohio State great Archie Griffin is the speaker at the Grid Iron Legend Luncheon at the College Football Hall of Fame. I sit down at the media table alongside Al Lesar of the *South Bend Tribune*.

Archie shares a story about when he was not famous. As a freshman at Ohio State in 1972, he was fifth string running back. Late in a blowout Coach Woody Hayes put him in a game. The quarterback pitched him the ball and Archie dropped it. Hello, bench.

The next week Ohio State played North Carolina. "The night before that game," Archie says. "I prayed to God that if I got to play that I play to the best of my ability." He got in the next day and rushed for an incredible 239 yards—an Ohio State record at the time. Remember, the week before he got in for one play and fumbled. Seven days later he came through with the greatest running back performance in Ohio State history. "To this day it has been the one miracle in my life," Archie says.

Archie admits at the luncheon that Ohio State used to spend *all* of spring practice preparing for the annual Michigan game. He says the Buckeyes spent *every* Monday during the regular season practicing on nothing but Michigan. And the week of the Northwestern game was spent *entirely* on Michigan (this was pre-Gary Barnett at Northwestern).

Archie emphasizes how much Woody Hayes pushed education at Ohio State. I can tell from the sincerity of Archie's voice that Woody meant business and really cared about his players future. "Coach Hayes had a saying that has stuck with me," Archie says. "An athlete without a good education is headed to a bad situation. I repeat, an athlete without a good education is headed to a bad situation."

FEBRUARY
Friday
27

The Pricker Doesn't Hurt Anymore and Rick Carter's Top 10 Indiana High School Basketball Games

It's time to roll up the sleeves and donate blood. The South Bend Medical Foundation Central Blood Bank is set up in the WSBT Conference room. Having signed up earlier in the week, I'm called down around 3. Fridays are the busiest day of the week for me but that doesn't matter in this case. Giving blood should be a priority for all of us who can.

Donna Payne, Diane Smith, and Diana Bayse (the three D's!) are still recovering from zany weatherman Rick Mecklenburg's morning donation. "He's so upbeat!" says Diana of the personable and very witty Mecklenburg.

They sit me down first to go over a series of questions about my physical self. As the questions are fired off, I tell myself that under no circumstances will I reveal that since turning 35 I have started growing hair on parts of my back. After assuring them I have had no body piercing, they prick me to check my blood.

Great News! The pricker doesn't hurt anymore. I couldn't stand the old way. Now they've got this device called Glucolet 2 which doesn't hurt at all. It's great for diabetics who have to check their blood regularly. Now that the pricker has been improved I'm ready to donate every six months. Donna tells me I have 41% red blood cells which is good. I feel like getting on the station P.A. system and bragging to everyone. My blood pressure is 126/80 which is very good. I find that amazing since we have two hyper kids at home. They say I have 60 pulse beats a minute. They should check me five minutes before the 11:00 Sports when three game highlight tapes have still not been edited. Donna tells me there is a "desperate need" for blood donation. I ask her why would people NOT donate blood since the whole process only takes 45 minutes. "People think it hurts and leaves them weak," says Donna. In my case, I go right back to work. I take it easy for a little bit, but it's not like I'm weak at all. "Some people also think they'll get A.I.D.'s," adds Donna. "But we use different equipment for every person. Everything is sterile." So get out and donate! If you want to give in St. Joseph County call them at (219) 234-1157.

For the past four years, I teamed up with Rick Carter to broadcast Indiana High School Basketball games for WSBT NewsTalk 960 radio. Rick has been the color commentator for the Martin's Super Markets Spotlight Games of the Week for 15 years. The North Liberty product has been courtside for some historic moments, so I asked him to list the top 10 High School Basketball games he has broadcast. Here's Rick, the Pride of North Liberty!

1) Clay vs. Valparaiso, 1994 State Championship game:
Miracle comeback! Future NBA players! Powerful individual performances! A last-second shot to send the thriller into overtime! This one had it all. Valparaiso's stars, Bryce Drew and Tim Bishop, were as magnanimous in defeat as they were magnificant on the court. Sophomore Jaraan Cornell overshadowed his 23 first-half points with a top of the key three-point basket for the tie at the buzzer. Clay coach Tom DeBaets pulled off one of the great coaching performances in the history of the tournament. This was a game, and a team, that the entire South Bend community could be proud of.
2) South Bend St. Joseph's vs. Marion, 1989 Semi-State morning game: Marion Coach Dan Gunn brought in a #1-ranked team that featured prolific scorer David Anderson and 6'6" Jody McCain. Missed free throws down the stretch allowed St. Joe to

erase an 11-point deficit with less than two minutes left. The Indians were down three with about seven seconds left in regulation, with four capable three-point shooters and center Kevin Lorton on the floor. The Giants, knowing this, blanketed everyone but Lorton. After several quick passes around the perimeter, the 6'5" center drilled a three from the corner. It was his only three-point attempt of the season. My partner, Lance McAlister, and I went absolutely ballistic! After the dust settled, feeling somewhat embarrassed after having momentarily lost my composure, I uttered the following apology: "Pardon my boyish enthusiasm, but that was the biggest shot I've ever seen!" St. Joe went on to win in overtime.

3) Concord vs. Bedford North Lawrence, 1990 State Championship game: *This will always be known as the Damon Bailey game. Playing in his third Final Four in four years, the man-child from Heltonville had already achieved legendary status. 41,046 witness this 63-60 B.N.L. victory. Damon was on the favorable end of a blocking call that could easily have been called a charge. Occurring late in the game, many feel this was the turning point. The Minutemen of Concord missed three last seconds three-point shots, losing in the final game for the second time in three years. Throughout this weekend, Damon continually referred to his teammates as kids, as in "the kids are playing real hard" or "I'm real proud of these kids." There seemed to be no way Damon would allow his team to lose.*

4) 1984 State Championship game between Warsaw and Vincennes: *Warsaw's team featured future Mr. Basketball Jeff Grose, 6'7" center Marty Lehman and Steve Hollar, who had a key role playing for the Hickory Huskers in the movie* Hoosiers. *My first State Championship game as a broadcaster saw the Tigers win a tight 59-56 contest at Market Square Arena.*

5) St. Joe vs. Concord, 1988 regular season: *This deserved to be ranked as one of the greatest high school sporting events in South Bend history. An overflow crowd filled the JACC to watch these two titans do battle. Even though the temperature hovered around zero, fans waited in line well past the scheduled tipoff, holding up the game for half an hour. Shawn Kemp led a*

Concord team that was destined to go to the State Finals. St. Joe was still a year away from their State Semi-Finals trip, but was still one of Indiana's best with players like Rodney Holmes, Darren Teamor, and Tom Corcoran. The game lived up to its billing, but Kemp and company were too much and won down the stretch.

6) Michigan City Rogers vs. Marion at Fort Wayne Semi-State in 1986: *The two best teams in Indiana squared off in a high scoring, competitive affair. Marion won in a cliffhanger after an errant last second in-bounds pass was intercepted and taken in by Marion for a breakaway layup and the final lead. Rogers coach Earl Cunningham had been heavily involved in a divisive teachers' strike and was threatened with incarceration. It had only been settled a few days before the Semi-State. The interim coach was Principal Doug Adams, who guided Elston to the 1966 State Championship game. Marion would go on to win the second of three straight State Championships.*

7) Riley vs. Valparaiso, first round of the 1990 Michigan City Regional: *Although team shooting statistics no longer exist, David Redmond of Valpo was 9-27 from three-point range. As a team, they hit 16 and shot close to 50 in the game. Bob Berger's Riley squad featured the likes of Eric Ford, Andre Owens, and Jermaal Sylvester. Four Wildcasts scored in the 20s. Valpo would up hitting a low percentage of their threes, giving the Wildcats an opportunity to do what they did best—get the rebound and run. Riley won, 112-100!*

8) Ben Davis vs. New Albany, 1996 State Championship game: *It went two overtimes! Jeff Poisel buried his sixth three of the game with two seconds left in the second OT for the 57-54 Ben Davis win. The shot was right in front of our courtside broadcast location. Play-by-play man Charlie Adams nearly lost his mind making the call of the final shot.*

9) Riley vs. Concord, 1990 regular season: *The interest in this game was so high that Riley moved it from Jackson Gym to Notre Dame's JACC. Both teams were state powers with championship potential. With Concord's great fan support and general community interest in the contest, the crowd numbered around*

7,000. The fans got their money's worth with Riley eeking out an 86-81 overtime win. Eric Ford poured in 37 and Concord's Jeff Massey had 28.

10) Warsaw vs. Michigan City Rogers, 1984 Fort Wayne Semi-State Championship game: *Rogers, led by Delray Brooks and his 33 ppg, was ranked #1 in the final poll. Warsaw was loaded as well and on its way to the State Championship. With Warsaw up by two, Rogers had a chance for the tie, but had time for only a full-court in-bounds pass and quick shot attempt. Brooks caught a three-quarter court throw, but missed an off-balance shot from the wing.*

—Rick Carter, WSBT NewsTalk 960 radio play-by-play for High School Basketball and color commentator for High School Football (Rick is also a regular on GameDay SportsBeat and WeekDay SportsBeat.)

The Joy of Reading

It's National Read to Kids Day. I drive out to Clay Middle School in South Bend after lunch to visit Cyndi Kingma's eighth grade class. She had written WSBT and invited me to read to her class. Since it's Dr. Seuss' birthday, Cindy has me read some of Doc's books. Before reading, I check to see if there's a wocket in my pocket. I have a lot of fun reading to students and appreciate their attentiveness and good manners. I then talk sincerely about the value of reading. It's very important that they make reading a key part of their lives. The U.S. Department of Education estimates there are over 40 million illiterate adults unable to read a newspaper, fill out a job application, or follow simple written directions.

Of all the first-class Notre Dame football players I've had the honor to cover at WSBT, Jim Flanigan certainly rates right up at the top of the list. The Chicago Bears defensive lineman founded the James Flanigan Foundation in 1997. It has stimulated interest in reading among thousands of young children. "I want children to understand that reading has helped me imagine things beyond what I would ever have known growing up in Wisconsin, going to school at Notre Dame, and playing pro football for the Bears," Flanigan told WSBT during his Great American Book Drive in 1998. "My life is rich, but it would not be nearly as rich without the worlds I have known and the things I have learned through reading. Reading and imagination go hand in hand, and imagination inspires hopes, dreams, and determination." (If you would like to support the non-profit Literacy for Life, James Flanigan Foundation, call 847-478-6802 or hit their web site at www.lit4life.org)

I tell the young students at Clay Middle School how my wife Sherrad and I read the *South Bend Tribune* early in the morning, how I enjoy reading magazines such as *Sports Spectrum,* and that I'm currently reading two books: *The Mind of Christ*, by T.W. Hunt, and *The Street Lawyer*, by John Grisham (when you have two kids under five constantly wanting you to play Grizzly Bear and chase them around the house, you tend to read books over longer periods of time).

"What's your favorite book?" a student asks.

"The Bible," I answer. I'm in a Sunday evening class at our church, Evangel Heights United Methodist, and right now we're going through the Bible in Disciple One. It meets basically every Sunday evening from 5 to 7:30 from August to May and has been a tremendous part of my spiritual growth this year. Between that and my Emmaus Walk in January, I am connecting with the Bible now more than ever before.

Among the students in the Clay Middle School class is Anthony Williams. He's basically blind with Retinitis Pigmientosis. Amazingly, Anthony played on the sixth grade basketball team three years ago at Darden. "He basically followed the sound of the basketball," Cyndi tells me after class. Anthony is the manager of the eighth grade team, which won the City Championship. He has a special teacher, Mrs. Court, who gets his lesson plans from teachers and types them into braille for him.

Back at WSBT I hop into an edit booth to put together the "Making a Difference feature." It's on Alice Black, a dynamic 80-year-old volunteer at Shamrock Gardens Assisted Living Facility. Activities Coordinator Suzanne O'Dell had called me the week before to ask me to do a story on Alice. "Alice comes in every day," says Suzanne. "I've heard more than one resident say that Alice is like being given an angel right here."

Perched in a chair, Alice leads the residents in regular Sitter-cize, which is light exercising while sitting down. Stiffness is the enemy of the elderly. This is an effective way for them to keep limbered up. Alice gingerly leads the residents through a variety of arm waves and leg raises. They stop often just to talk. The residents love Alice and it's obvious the feeling is mutual.

"I lost my husband Ralph about five months ago," Alice tells me. "These people are my support group. We're a lovely bunch of coconuts here."

I ask her about her giving spirit and the outpouring of love she shows for the residents. "It comes from the heart. I tell them you have to love yourself before you can love others." After Sitter-cize each morning, Alice takes them into the dining area for donuts and coffee. "She brings donuts everyday out of her pocket," Suzanne says. "Many times when the residents need something and she becomes aware of it, she's gone out and gotten it."

"Even when my husband was ill," Alice recalls, "he'd be driving me down here saying,'Keep doing this.' I just love people and doing for people." After spending the morning with the residents, Alice always heads to the Ironwood Rehab to be with her brother Albert Waumans. "I pray for strength," she says. "I'll keep doing this as long as I can, Charlie. I'm 80! How 'bout them apples! Wooooooooo! I'll go as long as the man upstairs tells me to go."

MARCH
Tuesday
3

Checking Out a Sportscasting Candidate

News Director Meg Sauer and I sit down in her office to talk about possibly hiring a woman sportscaster to do the sports on the 11:00 News. By taking me off the late news eventually, it will enable me to work dayside and concentrate more on "Making A Difference" segments. I'll co-anchor the 5:30 News and still do the sports at 6. I'm really excited about it because I'll be able to be at home at night with my family. Our five-year-old son Jack is entering Kindergarten while two-year-old Abigail has all sorts of questions about everything. I really want to be home as a parent at night. It's very important for families to be together at dinnertime so the kids can see Mommy and Daddy interact and everyone can talk about their day.

Donna Fendrick, weekend sports anchor at WMTV-TV in Portland, Maine, grabs our attention based on her resume tape. I'm all fired up for hiring a woman sportscaster. With the dynamic growth of women's sports in general, I think it will go over great. There's some concern that some male viewers may have a hard time with it. I agree that some ol' boys might go "harumph," but there have been so many good women sports-casters on ESPN and other national outlets lately that attitudes are chang-ing. We decide to meet again when we get another one of Donna's resume tapes. I'm anxious to see how this develops.

By now it's common knowledge in the newsroom that current morning weatherman Rick Mecklenburg is going to be the new chief meteorologist at WSBT, replacing Sam. This makes everyone happy, especially Sam. Here's Sam's account:

Rick reminds me of myself about seven years ago when I took over for Paul Silvestri. Keep in mind that I was only the third main weather person in WSBT-TV history, dating back to the early '50s: the legendary Bruce Saunders, then Paul, then me, and now Rick Mecklenburg. Rick is a professional meteorologist that will have a long career at WSBT and will serve the community well. WSBT never has and never will cut corners when it comes to weather technology. Especially, technology that could save lives. The new Storm Tracker and Storm Watch immediately show viewers where the worst storms are and where they are heading. It is this type of commitment from station management that will continue to make 22 WSBT the weather leader of the market. Also contributing to the safety of the community is northern Indiana's fairly new doppler radar system in Kosciusko County. I am so glad I had the opportunity to see the "official" commissioning of the radar the week before I left WSBT. Mike Sabones, Meteorologist in Charge, has a great team there in North Webster. As a community, you'll notice major improvements in service compared to what was coming out of the National Weather Service in Chicago.

Another man that I worked closely with in the WSBT Weather office was Bob Werner, Mr. Dependable. He means so much to weekend TV viewers. I tried for three years to get Bob to come over to WSBT from WNDU. He had been there for 17 years and had never once called in sick. For those of you who don't know, Bob works full-time at Notre Dame during the week. He's a remarkable forecaster. When Bob says a big storm is coming, rest assured it is!

—Sam Scaman

The controversial "Class Basketball" in Indiana starts tonight. The state tournament now has four classes instead of the "everyone in one tournament" that made Indiana famous. I anchor the 5 and 6 TV sports-casts live at Penn, sight of a 4-A Sectional.

Down at the Knox-Bremen Sectional game on this night. Geo Folkers of Knox makes a 70-foot basket at the end of a quarter in the game. WSBT's Brian O'Donnell gets the mighty heave on camera and it is quite a highlight on our popular high school basketball show, "Hoop It Up!"

Humiliating Co-Workers

On this day I will totally humiliate three WSBT workers. What better way to jazz up the middle of the work week. I've invited two recent champions to come in for another unpredictable "tour" of the WSBT Empire. One of our traditions is to invite state or national champions for a rather irreverent stroll around the WSBT building. The segments always turn out rather zany.

Over the past weekend in Indy, Penn's Olympic-caliber swimmer Jason Mallory won state championships in the 200 individual medley and set a state record in winning the 500 freestyle. Jason comes in with his parents, Tom and Lin, as well as Penn swim coach Rich Healy. I ask Jason, who is going to swim for Michigan, how he got so good. "It's my work ethic," he says in the storied WSBT lobby. "Everyone can come in and swim two hours. I think you have to do something while you're there and then put in extra effort. At the end, it pays off."

Also in for a "tour" is a remarkable youngster named Kevin Hart. The 10-year-old won the Gold Medal in the long jump competition at the AAU National Indoor Track and Field. After faulting on his first three jumps, Kevin came through with a leap of 11' 3" to win on his final jump. This is his birthday, which he shares with Knute Rockne. The fourth grader at St. Anthony's comes along with his proud dad, the sharply dressed Jim Hart.

I'm amazed at Kevin's athletic accomplishments in his young life:
- He has been a three-time winner of Local Punt, Pass, and Kick;
- He was Clay Team MVP in 1996 in Little League Baseball;
- He was on a 1997 Pop Warner championship team;
- He was seventh in state in AAU cross country;
- With relatives, he ran three legs in the Mount Rainier to the Pacific in the 155-mile race.

Kevin is a great sport as we zip around the building. He handles the TV interview well, which I attribute to the confidence he has gained from being active in sports.

As for humiliating three WSBT employees, I basically force two of our somewhat portly men to don swim trunks for a "bit" with Jason Mallory. 6:00 producer John Haferkamp, big Bob Green of the Production Department, and Jonathan (who is not portly) Miller of the Shipping Department, all look ridiculous in nothing but big swim trunks as Jason gives them swimming advice. When the segment airs at six, Mike and Cindy howl with laughter. Afterwards, in the News Room, News Director Meg Sauer gives me a hard time saying I'm going to run off all the female viewers showing such lumpy men. Poor Meg. She never knows what I'm liable to do in the sports segment. Meg goes way back at WSBT. A Penn High graduate (she went to school with current Warsaw Coach Al Rhodes), Meg worked her way up to be executive producer. She always did a great job. Just this past year she was promoted to news director and has given the demanding job everything she has. She's been like a Kingsmen defensive tackle pursuing the quarterback for Elkhart Central. Relentless. She has done an outstanding job of hiring people. I've never been around a better group of producers, reporters, and photographers in our newsroom. She has brought in people of character and integrity with passion. With hair longer than Crystal Gayle, she's easy to spot when I need to track her down about a pressing issue.

The nice surprise of the day comes in the evening when I'm editing a segment on Ricky Watters. The rather enthusiastic and onetime brash Irish running back has signed with Seattle. At his Seahawks news conference, Watters talks openly about asking Jesus to take over his life. He shares how big money and worldly possessions left him empty during his early NFL years and how Jesus has filled the void in his life. It's no doubt there's a growth of Christians in big-time sports. Claude Terry of Pro Basketball Fellowship tells *Sports Spectrum* magazine, "I believe it is just a work of God! I believe God is using sports figures as an example to the world that He is the answer."

Part Two
March 7-March 15, 1998

A Blow-by-Blow
Account of Everything
–and I Mean Everything That Happens in a Week

Here we go! For the next week *I'm going to "document" just about* everything *I do to try to give you an idea of what all happens during the course of a busy week. I'm going to take you from a Saturday evening to the following Saturday. You'll see some of the unpredictable things that affect me during the work week. You'll see why I had to sit in front of WSBT by myself in my car as everybody walked by and gave me strange looks. You'll get an idea of the decisions I have to make as sports director and the daily interaction I have with viewers and callers. I'll try to give you an idea of how a sportscast is put together and my family and spiritual life during one of the most challenging weeks of the sports year.*

SATURDAY EVENING MARCH 7

It's Sectional Championship night in Hoosier Hysteria (class basketball style). I'm doing the play-by-play for WSBT NewsTalk 960's radio broadcast (sponsored by Martin's Supermarkets) of the 4-A Final at Penn between Adams and Clay at 7:30. I meet color commentator Rick "Sergeant" Carter out at Penn at 5:30. The gym is quiet except for the sounds of Rick setting up our broadcast equipment on the second row. The teams have yet to arrive, so we shoot hoops for 20 minutes as officials line everything up for the big game. It brings back memories of covering the Michigan City Regional back in the late 1980s. After the morning games, several of us would play pick-up basketball on the court until the teams arrived for the championship game.

At 6:15, Penn assistant athletic director Teri Woodruff asks Rick and me to be three-point "test dummies." Within a half hour, there's going to be an IHSAA three-point contest between area high school sharpshooters. Penn wants Rick and me to give them a "dry run" so they'll be ready for the real thing. With ball racks and the whole works, Carter throws up a slew of bricks. It's obvious he is soon to turn 40 years old. I bury 10 in the allotted time. Not bad for a guy in khakis and a long sleeve shirt. The practice run-through helps Penn know they've got everything set for the high school competitors. Rod Ivory of LaSalle ends up winning the "real" contest. Rick and I settle in and slide on our headsets. The game begins and it's a rip-roarin' contest! The fans love it. Adams has brought a lot of spirited fans from the east side and they make so much noise that I have to press my headset close to my ear to hear Rick.

With 54 seconds left in the tight thriller, Clay's David Licini has to leave the game because of blood on his shorts. He can't come back in unless he has clean shorts on. Instead of running all the way to the lockeroom, Licini and a seldom used reserve dart under the bleachers where Licini takes off his shorts and puts on his teammate's. This is in full view of many fans. Licini rushes back to check back in the game. His teammate has the option of staying under the bleachers in his jock strap or donning the blood stained Licini shorts.

Adams wins, 70-65, in overtime in a game that's a joy to broadcast. For our postgame show I go onto the floor and get players such as Dan Sizemore, Lutfee Jennings, Barnbrook, and Mike Edwards to put on a headset and talk about Adams' first Sectional Title in 14 years.

As we go off the air, Adams poses for their team picture with the trophy. Edwards, who has been the subject of national and local media attention because he plays with an artificial leg, takes off his leg, and holds it above his teammates as the picture is taken. I can just picture someone visiting Adams 15 years from now and seeing that picture in the hallway!

It's been a fun Saturday night. I'm not doing anything on the TV News side, so I help Rick take down the radio equipment and then drive home. The impending storm of a wild work week that will see all sorts of curveballs thrown at me is just over 24 hours away.

SUNDAY MARCH 8

My wife Sherrad and I rise early to get the kids ready for church. By 8:45 AM we're at our church, Evangel Heights United Methodist, on Ironwood and Colfax. Pastor Ed Fritz (a Packers and Penn State football fan in those rare moments he's not studying Scripture) talks about Noah's Ark. What faith Noah showed when God told him to make the Ark. There wasn't a river within miles of where he built it. He worked on it for over 100 years! Never once did he question God's will or how he would rustle up all those animals. What an example of perseverance and patience.

After church service, I'm in Mike Jacob's Sunday School class. Mike is taking us through a 50-day program centered on Spectacular Energy Sources for the Body of Christ. As a Christian, sometimes there is suffering and pain. Mike can relate to that because Mike and his family have been season ticket holders to Notre Dame men's basketball in recent years. A discussion starts about the WWJD bracelets that are becoming very popular. There is concern the secular world is wearing them as somewhat of a hot trend, not treasuring the meaning of What Would Jesus Do. We go over being a 24/7 Christian: 24 hours a day. 7 days a week. Jesus didn't ask for those willing to follow him on the Sabbath, but for those who would take up his cross daily. Kent Alderton is visiting our class. He shares insight he gained on prayer from listening to a speaker at Wednesday night service. ***Prayer is rooted in praise. Nourished in honesty. Strengthened by obedience***.

Normally, we head home for lunch after Sunday school, but this week the church youth (the SonSeekers) have a mystery luncheon and musical for everyone in the Fellowship Hall. "The Secret of My Success" is a youth musical that teaches what God's Word says about true success. Trace Fritz has this line: "You know, God uses money in our lives as a tool, a test and a testimony. Our lives SHOULD testify that the richest people are those who have trusted Jesus."

At the end of the musical Doug Clements says, "Knowing Jesus Christ as your Lord and Savior will make you the richest person alive." Doug then reveals the secret to finding success. It's in Joshua 1:8 "Think about My words every day and every night so that you will be sure to obey them. For only then will you succeed."

After going home for a while to rest and spend time together, we come back to Evangel Heights in the early evening. Sherrad's in Disciple 3, which is an advanced study of the Bible. I'm in Disciple 1. Just about every Sunday 14 of us gather with the purpose of becoming Disciples through Bible study. Kent Alderton and Sonya Harrington lead our class. Tonight we're studying the explosive power of the Holy Spirit in Acts. Beth Ernsberger and I are asked to see how the Holy Spirit worked through the apostle Peter. I'm fascinated to learn that the sick were brought to the streets where they were healed by his passing *shadow*! In the reading, I see this statement: What the Church has always needed, perhaps more than anything else, is people who never care who gains the credit for it so long as the work is done.

During the break time of Disciple, Purdue fan Brad Varner and I talk about his beloved Boilermakers. They're going to be a high seed in the NCAA's. Brad tells me if he and his wife Marie have a third child and it's a boy, his name will be Joe Tiller Varner. If she's a girl then her name will be Josephine Tiller Varner.

As we drive home after Disciple, it hits me that the week ahead is going to be a load. It's like tax season for an accountant. The first week of March Madness is an adventure. The strength gained and spiritual replenishment gained from Sunday worship is so vital to me. Without it, facing the challenges of the work week ahead would eat me up.

MONDAY MARCH 9

Since I anchor the Sports at 5, 6 and 11:00, I obviously don't go into work in the early morning like most folks. As a family, we get up around 7. I have to have two cups of coffee immediately upon rising each morning or I will surely croak on the spot. I also have to microwave my coffee for 50 seconds, which Sherrad finds odd. We'll be visiting somebody and I have to put the coffee they offer me in their microwave. The hosts will look up and there I'll be in their kitchen touching microwave buttons.

Around 9 AM the phone rings and it's WSBT assignment coordinator John Snyder. The station is anxious to coordinate Friday's coverage of the Regionals in Hoosier Hysteria (Class Basketball style). We discuss where we should send the WSBT satellite truck. Perhaps Michigan City, where Adams will play LaPorte. Maybe the Warsaw Regional where Elkhart Central will meet Columbia City. By having the satellite truck on location, we can edit together a comprehensive game report and uplink it back to the station minutes before airtime. John and I discuss possibilities and plan to talk more when I get to the station later.

Having seen in the *South Bend Tribune's* "Worth Waking Up For" section that a local bookstore is having preschool reading time at 10 AM, Sherrad and I head towards Grape Road with Jack and Abby. As we walk in Jack starts angling for a toy and/or book. When I tell him we didn't bring much money, he quickly replies, "We can spend short money." That's his perception of buying something inexpensive. The kids listen to book readings about ABC's and 1 2 3's. Seeing an opening, Sherrad leaves me in the kids section to watch Jack and Abby while she looks at books. We then head over with the kids to Pinnacle where Sherrad and I get in a brisk 50-minute workout. Regular exercise is so important, especially with a stressful week like this ahead of me. After huffing and puffing, we're back home by noon. The phone rings. It's newsroom secretary Jennifer Addington. Arrangements are being made for us to cover Purdue in the NCAA Tournament this coming Friday night. The Boilers will be playing the first two rounds in Chicago. She wants to know if I would go or if I will send someone else. I tell her I'll decide by the end of the day.

My so-called work hours are 2:30 to 11:30, but rarely do I start exactly at 2:30. Today, I get to WSBT at 1:15 because there are a lot of things to line up for the week. I sometimes refer to Monday's as my "administrative" day as sports director. I check my voice mail first. Joe Pate of the IHSAA has called wanting to know what Regional game we'll be doing on AM 960 radio. Lee Owens, sportscaster at a Jackson, Mississippi, TV station, has called to ask us if we will be interviewing Valparaiso players this week. He would like us to send him those via satellite because Valpo is playing Mississippi in the NCAA Tournament on Friday. I call him back to tell him we will try to get over there, but can't guarantee it. It's ironic that at the time I have no idea of the magical run that Valpo is about to make. There's no sense of urgency on my part to get a crew over there because they've lost in the first round of the NCAA's the past two years. On this day, there aren't many sports fans in America who know about Homer and Bryce Drew. Boy, is that about to change!

The worst snowstorm of the winter is blasting away outside. Inside the newsroom, producers huddle and coordinate extensive weather coverage. They alert me I'll be getting less time at 5 and 6 for Sports so they can emphasize weather coverage.

I log on and check the Associated Press wire on the computer. The Bears' Alonzo Spellman has holed up in his publicist's house in Chicago. He's upset that the NFL wants him to take a steroid test. There's one story for the 5 and 6 sportscasts.

An URGENT comes across the wire. Bob Knight has appealed the Big Ten's decision to suspend or fine him for going ballistic in the Illinois game. I jot that down as another story, obviously, to have on. It will probably lead the 5. I then decide that NASCAR's rain-delayed Primestar 500 in Atlanta will be the third story at 5.

Having received no formal nominations for Athlete of the Week (the snow has closed many schools), I call Adams coach Pat King to ask him if he thinks guard Armando Femia would be a good choice. He enthusiastically agrees, noting that Femia is probably the top male athlete of the sports year at Adams. We line up Wednesday at 3 to tape the feature. I ask him to fax over a bio on Femia for background information for our radio and TV "Athlete of the Week" spots. I then call Thom Jeiger in Sales and let him know who the Athlete of the Week will be. Thom takes a short break from reading *Green Bay Packers Digest* and orders the plaque.

I bound upstairs to check the mail. There's several pamphlets hyping high school basketball players for Mr. or Miss Basketball. One is from LaPorte touting Greg Tonagel (what a classy kid he is). Another is from Bluffton hyping Abby Salscheider.

I hustle back downstairs to write the scripts for the 5:00 Sports. I'm getting two minutes and 20 seconds of sportscast time, so the Knight story will get about 50 seconds. The Spellman incident, which is still developing, about :30, and the NASCAR highlights will get about :40.

The phone rings. Benton Harbor calls to say District games are postponed that night because of snow. As soon as I hang up, Dan Lucy of KOLR-TV in Springfield, Missouri, calls. His station is going to Lubbock, Texas, to cover their team, Southwest Missouri State, against the Notre Dame women. He wants us to split the $300-a-day satellite bill Texas Tech is charging them to edit and uplink from its satellite down there. In return, he will zap us coverage of Notre Dame. I tell him our News Director Meg Sauer will have to approve.

The phone rings again. It's sports reporter Matt Burridge. He's stuck in traffic behind a wreck on the 20 Bypass. He doesn't know when he'll get in. This poses a problem. I'm counting on him to edit a feature for the 6:00 Sports. I'm about to head to the Center for the Homeless to tape a "Making a Difference" story. If Matt doesn't make it in, then I'm going to have to scramble like heck to put the 6:00 Sports together. Matt grew up in Goshen and got his Communications degree at Butler University in Indianapolis. He's been our weekend sports anchor and weekday sports reporter for the last four years. It's very special to Matt to be able to cover sports in this area since he grew up here. He's one of the most dependable people I've ever been around. Matt does a lot of behind the scenes work on WSBT's popular shows "Friday Night Fever" and "Hoop It Up."

At 2:50, photographer Jason Scheuer and I go to the Center to tape the feature. It's to be on Deb Southworth, who makes birthday cakes the homeless children request. When we get there, Sarah Badger—development coordinator of the Center for the Homeless—tells us Deb is delayed because of the snowy roads.

Oh oh. This isn't good. I'm cutting it close as it is. I have not written one thing for the 6:00 Sports yet. I have to be back in the Sports office by 4:00, especially if Matt isn't able to make it in. We wait anxiously until 3:40. I tell Sarah that unless Deb makes it within five minutes I'll have to reschedule. I really don't want to because it's such a nice story, but the deadline clock is ticking. In four minutes, 60 seconds before my self-imposed deadline of leaving, Deb walks in with a Princess Diana cake for a child. We tape everything we need in 20 minutes and get back to the station by 4:05.

Now I'm scrambling! But the phone keeps ringing! A parent calls to tell me the Irish Youth Hockey League championship game is Thursday night and we should be there. The next call is from a former WSBT'er Sage Steele, who is now a sports anchor/reporter at WISH-TV in Indy. She is going to Valparaiso to do a story on the Crusaders and asks me for some background information. I rave about Coach Homer Drew and star Bryce Drew. Sage has a tremendous future in this business. Tall, intelligent, attractive, the sky's the limit for her.

At 4:20 I run to the hall of edit suites to put together the sports tapes. Argh! Every one is filled with reporters editing weather coverage. In situations like this, I ask each person, "Is your stuff for the 5 or 6?" Since I am pressed to get my stuff edited for the 5, as soon as I come across someone editing for the 6, I will tell them to get their butt out of the booth. They can edit their stuff later. Soon, I oust a reporter and plop into an edit booth to "splice" together the NASCAR highlights on one tape. I edit some file tape of Knight on another. These are taken back to the main editing room. They will take them upstairs to the person that rolls tapes during the news. At 4:40 I trudge into the restroom to put on makeup. Man, do I hate this part of the day. I slap on some pancake foundation and then some powder to take away the "shine" on my forehead. I poof up my brillo hair and then zip back into the sports office. I am not known as one who makes a big effort to pretty myself up.

At 4:50, Operations Manager Bob Johnson pops in to tell me he played Erskine with erratic golfer/hacker Luke Choate on Saturday. He suggests we do a feature on the man's backyard near the seventh hole. "There's all sorts of balls in his yard," Bob says. "You should interview him about that." I make a mental note to do just that one of these days.

The 5:00 News starts. Matt has made it in despite the snow. At 5:05, I have him call WBBM-TV in Chicago to get information on the Spellman story. I call WISH-TV in Indy to get more on the Knight story. Their producer tells me a ruling on Knight's appeal is expected around midweek. Matt then relays me what WBBM says about Spellman. WBBM has crews at the house Spellman is holed up in, so they have a lot of information.

At 5:10, I go into the computer and rewrite my 5:00 scripts with the information I've learned on both stories. I reprint the scripts and have an intern bring me the new copies moments before going on the set to anchor the 5:00 Sports. As I sit down during the commercial before Sports, co anchor Debra Daniel asks me what my lead story is. That gives her an idea of how to start the "chit chat" at the beginning of Sports. I fly through the sportscast. Luke and Debra listen intently as I tell about the bizarre Alonzo Spellman story.

Despite being stuck behind a wreck for part of the afternoon, Matt is able to edit his feature for 6. It's a neat story on the boys' basketball players at St. Mary's of Assumption. Since their season has ended, they decided to support the girls team by becoming cheerleaders. Once Matt is finished editing the 1:06 feature, I edit in a Flash Frame of Latrell Sprewell into the end of his feature. I'm not crazy about putting that yahoo in as Flash Frame, but I'm pressed for time. Normally, I cruise through various channels on our satellite and tape a shot of a celebrity like Boss Hog from "Dukes of Hazzard," Cannon, Denzel Washington, or Mickey Rooney for Flash Frame. The "flash" of the celebrity is only about one-third of one second long. The first caller that identifies the Flash Frame wins all sorts of prizes.

Having printed out the 6:00 Sports scripts by 5:50, I go back into the office and begin planning Friday's Regional coverage. So many viewers perceive my job as mainly "sportscasting" but 75% of it is lining up stories and running the Sports Department. It's a challenging task. I can never stop planning for the days ahead. I start tinkering with which photographers will go to what Regionals. It's somewhat like a general deciding how to dispatch his troops in battle. I strategize how we will get Regionals in seven sights covered with five photographers. I do this up until 6:15 when I head out to the studio to anchor the 6:20 sports. Back in the newsroom, 11:00 producer Jim Pinkerton mans the phone for Flashframe. As soon as Sprewell pops up for one-third of a second, the phones start ringing. Mike Haller of Niles guesses Sprewell. Jim tells him over the phone a College Football Hall of Fame hat and T-shirt will be in the WSBT lobby for him to pick up during the week. Mike says he'll give them to his son Josh, who will be a fine tight end and defensive lineman for the Niles High School football team.

Most nights after the 6:00 News I would go home and spend an hour and a half with Sherrad and the kids. With the snow getting worse, I call Sherrad and we decide it's best I stay at the station. As I hear Abby howl in the background, I just know Sherrad is excited about getting no help with the kids that night! I was going to have Matt cover the District basketball playoff game at Niles, but I don't want him to have to battle the increasing snow later at night driving to his home in Goshen. I tell Matt to head on home now. We'll just show a score of the Niles-Edwardsburg game instead of highlights. Before Matt leaves, we talk about what he'll do tomorrow. I tell him to take a camera and gear home with him to Goshen. Tomorrow, he'll go to Bethany Christian and Fairfield High Schools to interview their coaches and players on their upcoming Regional games. I tell Matt to also call Elkhart Central in the morning and try to swing by Dean Foster's practice to get their thoughts on their Regional game against Columbia City. I tell Matt the last thing he'll do Tuesday night is shoot some highlights of the Lakeshore-St. Joseph District playoff game at Niles.

Back in the Sports office at 7:30, I play the latest voice mail. A Ball State fan named Leon "B" has left an angry message wanting me to investigate why Ball State didn't make the NCAA Tournament.

I call Lee Owens back in Jackson, Mississippi, to tell him we probably won't go to Valpo. I suggest he call Sage in Indy to get a copy of her interviews.

Recognizing the weather coverage will still be top priority for the 11:00 News, I send an e-mail to 11 PM producer Jim Pinkerton suggesting he cut my sports back from four minutes to three so they can have more time. This is what being a team player is all about. Helping others. On a Friday night, Jim gives me a ton of extra time.

I go through more mail. Sue Artusi of Mishawaka High wants me to speak at Career Day in late April. I check my calendar and write them back that I will be there. I then make the decision that I should be on-sight Friday for Purdue's NCAA Tourney opener in Chicago. I e-mail secretary Jennifer Addington to get our credentials. Since I will be at the Purdue game, I'll miss doing the play-by-play radio for AM 960's broadcast of the Michigan City Regional Friday night. I call Rick Carter and ask him to line up former Riley coach Bob Berger to work with him on the Adams-LaPorte game.

For the 11:00 sportscast, I put together a piece on the opponents that Purdue, IU, Michigan, Michigan State, Valpo, and Butler will face in their NCAA openers. This gives fans a feeling for what their favorite team will be up against. The top stories of the day are also included. Around 10, I go down the hall and record morning sports reports that will air on Sunny 101.5 FM and WSBT NewsTalk 960. I also put together a TV Sports "Wrap" that will run on the WSBT-TV morning news. By 11:00 I've got everything done. I wander into the newsroom where I see that Executive Producer Tim Ceravolo has left his computer on. With 15 minutes to kill before doing sports, I plop down at the terminal and go to work. I admit it. I'm a compulsive "get on somebody's computer and send e-mail" prankster. To weekend weatherman Bob Werner, I send this:

> *Bob—In an effort to get younger viewers, we would like all our weekend anchors to appear to be 30 years old or younger. Obviously, you are into your 40s. At station expense, we would like to get you some hair lotions to take the gray out. We would also like you to firm up and take off some pounds. From: Tim.*

Zap. I send that to Bob. I can't wait for him to overreact. I then come up with a doozy to our three "beat" reporters Ray Roth (Marshall and surrounding counties), Robert Borrelli (Elkhart County), and Roszell Gadson (Michigan).

This is what I type out from Tim's terminal:

> *ROLE CHANGES.*
> *From: Tim Ceravolo*
> *To: Roth, Borrelli, Gadson.*
> *In a move that I think you all will find exciting and challenging, we are going to change your beat responsibilites. I feel this will recharge you all and give you each fresh territory to cover. Effective June 1, Ray will take over the Michigan beat. Roszell will handle Elkhart County, while Robert will move to Marshall and surrounding counties. The transitions will be smooth to allow each beat reporter to share accumulated information, contacts, and files. I will meet with you individually and as a group. Tim.*

Keep in mind Ray has lived in Plymouth his whole life. If this really happened he would have to move to Michigan. Zap. I send the e-mails. I can just picture Ray Roth going through the roof in the morning and calling Tim. Tim will be like, "What are you talking about, Ray? And please, calm down. I can't understand you because you are screaming."

Because Tim is a recent hire, as executive producer he can make these "decisions." I slide away from Tim's computer anxious to see what reactions these get tomorrow.

After the 11:00 News, I get home about 11:45. In preparation for Sunday's Disciple class, I read Acts 15:36 to 18:28. It is about Paul going to Macedonia. I also read from 1st Timothy for a Sunday School lesson. Since my Emmaus Walk in January, I have read and learned so much more from the Bible. Ending the day by reading Scripture puts me in a very peaceful state as I climb into bed. For years, I used to come home after the 11:00 News and mindlessly flip through the channels. After my Emmaus Walk, that changed. Now I want to end the day reading the Word.

TUESDAY MARCH 10

Sherrad is up early to watch the WSBT morning news. She is anxious to see what is closed because of the snowstorm. Abby ended up rooting out a warm, cozy spot in our bed during the night. She and I wobble downstairs around 7. I generally get about six hours of sleep a night during the time of the year when we do the 11:00 news. I could sleep in longer, but I want to see Sherrad and the kids before they head off to the pre-school where Sherrad teaches. Oh, how I yearn for April when we start doing the 10:00. I'll get to bed at a more decent hour.

Sherrad's job is snowed out, so we chill out at home. Jack and Abby and I go down in the basement. I'm Godzilla. Jack is Rap-tar. He claims, as Rap-tar, he can fire something at me that "pins me to the wall." I tell him I have a "force field." Ha! Jack doesn't miss a beat. He quickly informs me he has a zapper that breaks force fields. I never can get the best of Jack in these games. five-year-olds are too clever! As a two-year-old, Abby does whatever Jack does. She calls him Jacky.

I was supposed to go to Cleveland Elementary School and read to the kids this morning. Ellen Ehmer had invited me. The snow has whited that out. When I get into work I'll call them to see if they want me to come back later in the week. Over lunch, I read some of Ken Davis' book entitled *Fire Up Your Life*. I'm always looking for insight from Christian authors.

On this day, the Bears' Alonzo Spellman is continuing his bizarre behavior. They ended up taking him to a mental hospital after Monday's incident. Today, in freezing weather, Spellman has marched out of the place in nothing but pants. It would be easy to write some witty copy for the news, but instead I worry about him. What's going through his head? I hope he's not thinking of doing something to himself.

At WSBT, I run into Bob Werner in the Weather office. "Have you ever thought about darkening your hair to look younger?" He looks at me seriously, like something has been on his mind. "It's ironic you should say that, Charlie. Tim wants me to." I tell Bob that *I* sent that message.

He breathes a big sigh of relief. "Oh, man, Charlie! I had been wondering all morning how I was going to respond to Tim. At my age, that's actually a message I've been thinking I would get." There's no reaction to the "beat switch for Roth/Borrelli/Gadson" message. I called newsroom secretary Jennifer Addington early this morning to have her send all three men an e-mail saying it was a joke. Ray Roth might have read it upon getting to his Plymouth bureau office, gone ballistic, and called up Tim and said, "I quit before I leave my beat!! I've lived here my whole life. How can you expect me to cover Michigan? What!? Do I get a house up there?"

In the newsroom, Executive Producer Tim Ceravolo says there's been a change in plans for the week. Instead of me going to Chicago to cover Purdue, they'd rather me stay here and host a special late night edition of "Hoop It Up." CBS' NCAA Tournament coverage will go until about 12:30 AM Friday night. Instead of us doing a routine newscast at that late hour that not many people would stay up to watch, they'd rather us do a basketball show emphasizing the Regional Championships that night. What the heck. The audience at that hour will be basketball fans. We'll have fun with it and get a lot of coverage in. Immediately, I start running ideas through my head as to how to produce the show—what elements to put in.

Back in Sports the phone rings. It's Niles High School athletic director Bob Ballentine. Snow has caused them to postpone that nights games. He asks me to announce that and to tell viewers when they will be made up. I hang up and immediately write a story on that for the 5:00 sportscast. Ring! Matt calls in. He has been to Bethany Christian and Fairfield to get interviews on upcoming Regional games. He tells me Elkhart Central is not available because they're going to Warsaw to acclimate to their 4-A Regional sight. Matt tells me he's going to Northridge instead to interview the Raiders about their game with Plymouth Friday. I tell Matt when he gets back to cut me three separate vo/sots that I will run over the next two days. A vo/sot is where I "voice-over" some video and then stop talking as the SOT comes up. That stands for "sound on tape." Vo/sots generally run about 10 seconds of "vo" and 20 seconds of SOT.

The phone rings constantly with folks wanting to know which NCAA Tourney first-round games WSBT will be televising Thursday and Friday. I hustle upstairs and meet with Programming Director Julius DeCocq. He has been in constant contact with CBS. Some games we'll televise are no-brainer decisions, like games involving Indiana and Purdue. The station would be burned to the ground if we didn't show them (when IU-Michigan was not televised three years ago because the Daytona 500 ran long, we got "the big red rampage"—hundreds of angry calls from IU fans). Julius gives me a list of the Thursday games we'll televise. Friday's coverage will start with Valparaiso-Mississippi at 12:20. For the 2:30 slot, we wrestle with whether to show TCU (with Clay High grad Lee Nailon) or the Butler University game. Butler is an Indiana school with two local players (Riley's Mike Pflugner and NorthWood's Andy Hirschy). We decide on Butler. Friday night's 7:30 game will be Purdue-Delaware. "We'll get angry calls from Michigan fans," Julius says, "because their game is on at the same time. But what can we do? CBS will do cut-ins to their game." There are options as to what game we'll televise Friday at 10:00 PM. The St. Johns-Detroit game looks good but we decide on Radford-Duke. Why? Radford is led by Bremen's Corey Reed, who is an Academic All-America and a very skilled basketball player.

When I get back downstairs, I write a story for the 6:00 Sports on what games we'll televise. Ring! I pick up the phone and a lady immediately starts pleading with me to air Butler because her grandson is on their cheerleading squad. I tell her she's in luck. Butler will be on. She likes that answer. I feel bad about Nailon and TCU, but chances are they'll win their first rounder and be on CBS over the weekend. Butler will be one and out.

During the 5 Sports, the teleprompter goes out. As the piece on Michigan State airs, I pick up the set phone and call producer Jerry Siefring in the control booth upstairs. I get testy and ask what happened. He doesn't know yet, but will report it in a discrepancy report. It's just one of those things. When the teleprompter (the words we read are in the screen) goes out, you rely on your paper script copy that you bring to the set. Your head bobs up and down as you look at that blank screen in the camera where normally the words of your script appear. It's no big deal. Half the time I ad lib my sports anyway. It's just as an anchor you don't like "surprises" like the teleprompter going out in the middle of sports.

Walking back to the Sports office, BING, an idea hits me. Since we're doing the Friday night "Hoop It Up" show about 12:40 AM, I should host it in a bed. I'll wear pajamas and have some fun with the fact it's so late. Now I have to get that approved by Meg and the other decision makers. My power of persuasion usually works in these matters. What is especially effective is that I don't take no for an answer. Eventually I wear them down (bug them to death to where they say, "Go Away! Just do it!").

During the 6:00 News, my "Making a Difference" feature airs on Deb Southworth. She is the lady who has been making elaborate birthday cakes for children at The Center for the Homeless and the Hope Rescue Mission. She recently left nursing after 20 years. "I prayed for a year and a half if God had another way for me to serve Him," she says in the story. "I was watching Oprah's Angel Network and tried to figure out what I could do for our community to make things a little better. It's Cakes for Kids!" I teach cake making, so with my abilities I started making whatever cakes the children wanted. I wanted the children to know how valuable they are. They are really special." Deb wants to branch out to make cakes at The Women's Shelter and the YWCA. She needs a small building to be able to do this. Cakes for Kids is a non-profit operation. If you would like to help, call 219-288-2213.

After anchoring the 6:00 Sports, I call the Flash Frame winner at his home. Rick Denny of South Bend was first to name Jamie Lee Curtis. Rick's an academic advisor at IUSB. He tells me the key to getting flash frame is "not to blink during sports." I congratulate Rick and tell him a brand new hat and shirt from the College Football Hall of Fame will be at the front desk for him.

I then head home where Sherrad has made her delicious spaghetti with sauce that is out of this world. Jack and Abby both have colds, so

Sherrad and I bear-wrestle them to the floor to make them take cough medicine. Jack then brings me a book to read to him. It's *The Stinky Cheese Man* and other *Fairly Stupid Tales (like the Really Ugly Duckling)*. It's a strange book, but Jack's a nut, so it's right up his alley.

Back at the station I get a fax from Purdue. It has their itinerary while in Chicago for the NCAA first and second round. It is detailed to the minute. It says their pep rally is Friday from 4:00 to 5:15 at the Sheraton Towers, so I make a mental note that Mike Stack could go live from there for the 5:00 Sports Friday. The fax says that unless you've been notified, you've been cleared to cover their NCAA Tournament games. Little do I know I will get a "surprise" change on that within 24 hours.

At 8:45 PM, WISH-TV sports producer Jimmy Shumar calls from Indianapolis. He is one of the nicest sports producers I've ever dealt with. He asks if we have gone to Valparaiso this week. I tell him I thought Sage Steele of his station was going. He says she had to cover another story. I tell him we couldn't have gone if we wanted because of the weather. He tells me they need something because they're doing an hour special Wednesday night incorporating all teams from Indiana in the NCAA's.

I think for a minute. Jimmy can hear the rocks in my head sifting as I actually think. "Jimmy," I say, "how about we send you a feature Matt Burridge did on Bryce Drew last month? It's a great interview and would be even better than typical clichè comments Valpo would have on Mississippi." Jimmy likes that idea so I tell him I'll leave the tape for our assignment editor John Snyder. John will uplink it via satellite tomorrow morning to the Mideast Feed which WISH tapes every day. In my mind, WISH-TV is one of the top stations in America. Their news director Lee Giles runs a wonderful news organization. They help us all the time by sending us interviews they do at Purdue and Indiana, so I try to help them anyway I can.

At 10:00 News anchor Cindy Ward comes into the office. An URGENT has come across the wire. The Big Ten has rejected IU's appeal of their punishment of Bob Knight. "We're teasing that in headlines," Cindy says. "Teasing" means that at 10:58, right before the 11:00 news, Cindy will say, "Coming up, late breaking developments in the Bob Knight story." That "teases" the viewer into staying up and watching. Actually, Cindy will write something better than "late breaking developments." Cindy and Mike Collins can write 10 times better than I can. They really know how to craft a story. Me, I just get out there and bellar for four minutes. My idea of brilliant writing is, "The Bulls took on the Miami Heat tonight."

The always-enthusiastic Mike Stack comes back in. He's been in Michigan covering District Basketball playoff games. "Do you want me to put a bite from the Bridgman coach on the end of the highlights of the Bridgman-Buchanan game?" he asks.

"Sure," I reply. "Get me the times when you can." I'm banging out the 11:00 scripts and I need to know the times so I can write that information down for the director. Stack calls back from the edit booth in 10 minutes. "The highlights run :29. The coach comes up at :30. The outcue is :43." "What's the outcue," I reply. "Real pleased," Stack says. I write that in the script. That way the director knows the tape ends at :43 when the coach says "real pleased."

The national sports feed is coming down via satellite. Once the Bulls' highlights are sent from CBS Newspath feed, I take them and a Gene Keady interview tape back into editing. I cut three Bulls' plays and then a :15 comment from Keady on Delaware. Stack comes back into Sports to pursue Michigan District scores. I go down the hall and cut AM and FM radio wraps. I talk about the Big Ten rejecting IU's appeal and all the games WSBT-TV will televise.

At 10:45, with the 11:00 Sports all done, I sit down and make my picks for the Indiana All-Star girls' basketball team. As a member of the media, I get a ballot form. I look through all the candidates and pick the incredible Kelly Komara of Lake Central as my vote for Miss Basketball. She devoured Penn last year in a game that left Penn coach Dominic Ball breathless in praise of her. I also vote for local players Tiffany Ross of Warsaw, Brooke Crawford of Lakeland, and LoriDawn Klotz of NorthWood for All-Stars. Those pamphlets I've been getting made these picks possible.

The 11:00 Sports goes fine. Rick Carter, who is also a director, and the crew in the booth do their usual flawless job of punching all the right buttons. During the highlights of Brandywine and River Valley, the floor director gives me the two-minute cue (time left in Sports). Within a split second, while talking about the Brandywine game, my brain has to tabulate how much sports I have left in my show. I know I have a :45 story on the Fairfield Falcons, about :40 of Michigan scores, and a :45

piece on Notre Dame hockey. That's more than two minutes, so instead of showing five plays from the Brandywine game, I say, "lets see the Michigan scores" after three plays. That will save :15. I then fly through the Michigan scores which saves another :15. That way I can get in Fairfield and ND hockey. Otherwise, I would have had to drop hockey from the sportscast. The director, Rick Carter, can sense when I speed up and knows I'm accelerating the pace to get the last story in.

Upon getting home, with Sherrad and the kids resting peacefully, I continue my Disciple One preparation by readings Acts 19 and 20. In verse 35 of Chapter 20 Paul says, "We must help the weak, remembering the words the Lord Jesus himself said: 'It is more blessed to give than to receive.'" God did incredible things through Paul. People touched him with handkerchiefs and aprons and then took those things to the sick. For Sunday School preparation, I read from 1 Peter. In Chapter 4, the apostle Peter writes, "Above all, love each other deeply, because love covers over a multitude of sins."

WEDNESDAY MARCH 11

After my obligatory two cups of coffee and *South Bend Tribune*, I help the kids get ready for preschool. This is Sherrad's one day of the week away from the kids, so she strongly suggests I leave the house so she can have some quiet time. Sherrad is a wonderful mother (and wife!—I better put that in this book) who tends to their every need. Like any adult, though, she needs time totally to herself, so Wednesday mornings it's my job to get out of Dodge.

I've got a 10 AM appointment in Elkhart with C.P.A. Gail Nilsson of Burnham and Beyler Public Accountants. They do our tax preparation each year. I admire accountants, their knowledge of math is astonishing. Me? I had a hard time passing Math for Elementary Teachers when I was an Education major at Ole Miss. It's ironic that March is their tax season—their busy time. March is also our "tax" season because of Hoosier Hysteria and March Madness. This is our craziest and most demanding month also.

After running some errands, I get into WSBT about 2:30. I see Bruce Leckband of TV Operations in the hallway. "Bruce!" I say, "You've got to get a bed for the studio. I really want to anchor the late, late Friday night 'Hoop It Up' in pajamas!"

"You are serious?" the University of Iowa grad answers.

"Yes! I've just got to work on Meg a little more."

Bruce promises to look into it. He says he had heard about this but thought it was a joke.

In the office, I play phone messages. Adams coach Pat King says since the weather was so bad in Michigan City, they missed their scheduled practice at the Michigan City gym yesterday, so they're going there today to get acclimated to the Regional site. I'm thankful he called because Mike Stack was going to Adams to interview them. Mike walks into the office. "How about you go to Michigan City and do a story about them walking in gawking at the size of the gym?" I ask. I like to pitch ideas by Mike and Matt instead of saying YOU WILL DO THIS all the time. Mike agrees enthusiastically. He is a very creative reporter. His imagination wheels start to click in his head. "Am I still going to shoot highlights of the District at Niles?" he says. "No. You concentrate on doing a package on Adams. I'll request a news photog to get up there." Mike leaves and I play the phone messages again. I'm stunned to hear Purdue Athletic Department official Jim Vruggink say the NCAA has denied the requests of South Bend stations WSBT and WNDU and Elkhart station WSJV to cover the NCAA games in Chicago. Jim says the NCAA is enforcing a rule where media outlets have to cover (in person) 90% of a team's home games in the regular season to cover them in the NCAA's. I can't stand dealing with the NCAA. I march into the newsroom to confer with Meg and Tim. They tell me they've been on the phone with CBS and Purdue trying to get the decision changed.

Upstairs, I grab the *Golf Digest* out of my mailbox and give it to erratic golfer/hacker Luke Choate. He gets all excited because he thinks he'll learn more about the physics of the swing. My father once told me, "Son, those golf magazines want to get you so confused that you keep reading them to try to get your swing figured out."

In the Sports office, Rick Carter tells me he's concerned AM 960 won't be able to do the Adams-LaPorte game on radio as scheduled. "They haven't been able to get a phone line in the gym," Rick says. "It's been closed because of the snow." I have no idea what I could do to help the situation. I don't have phone equipment and a big sagging leather belt with tools and phone lines, so I just nod and empathize with Rick. It will get worked out. Director Pat McGovern bounces in. He reminds me the deadline is near for entries into the NCAA pool. I plop down and make my picks in the bracket. A sports director's worst nightmare is bombing with his picks because Pat posts everyone's progress on the main bulletin board. I can just picture Elaine at the front desk doing better than I do. I tab Kansas, the alma mater of former WSBT'er Jim Cohn, to win it all.

I get an e-mail from Nancy TenBroeck. She handles publicity for the St. Joseph County Public Library. She thanks me for the "Making a Difference" story on the Special Services Department. She writes that the library always appreciates WSBT's efforts. On the newsroom wall e-mails are posted from viewers complimenting the weather coverage of the week.

The new book, *Pioneers of the Hardwood*, has arrived. I'm going to give that away to the Flash Frame winner today. It documents the early days of pro basketball in Indiana. Todd Gould wrote it. Indiana University Press published it. I had called the publisher a few days ago and told them I would publicize the book as a Flash Frame giveaway.

Ring! It's T.J. Shidaker, a 10th grader at Buchanan High School. He has asked me to bring the WSBT Charity basketball team up April 29th to raise money for their Police Explorers' program. He needs to know what players we'll be bringing so they can make a roster. Norm Stangland is always there. I also tell him to put down Angela Ganote, Paul Kiska, Bob Werner, Bob Montgomery of AM 960, Rick Mecklenburg and a few others. I tell him to put down Bethel star Rico Swanson and Notre Dame's Derek Manner. I'm going to call Derek to see if he'll play with us a few games. I tell T.J. that I'll be playing.

"You do Sports, don't you?" he asks.

Ahhh! Nothing like being well known.

I call Bethany Christian High School to tell them at 5:00 we're running a piece on the Bruins winning their first Sectional. Administrative assistant Betty Yoder is excited. She says she'll spread the word. Then when I go to write the story I find I can't read Matt's writing. I call Betty back to see if a players last name is "Shrock" or "Shruck." It's Shrock.

Around 4:00 I write out the 5:00 and 6:00 sportscasts. URGENTS have come across saying Bob Knight will pay a $10,000 fine. Both sportscasts will lead with that. On the computer I see that Knight will talk at 6:15 at their NCAA press conference in Washington, D.C. I give the satellite coordinates (SBS 6/Transponder 4) to producer Jim Pinkerton. He processes paperwork to get to Engineering so that we can tape that as it happens live.

Ring! It's Rick Wood, pastor at Grace Baptist. He tells me they have a tournament Thursday night at Goodman Auditorium at Bethel. I tell Rick that we may or may not come out.

"Rick, since the NCAA Tourney is on CBS, our 11:00 News Thursday night won't go on until about 12:45 AM. Hardly anyone would see the highlights." I try to be honest with folks as to whether we can be at their event or not. Normally, we'd be there in a heartbeat.

I check voice mails again. An IU fan named Joe Hopkins wants me to call him at work when I know something about the Knight story.

Around 4:45, I see Meg in the hall and start bending her ear about me anchoring the Friday night, late, late "Hoop It Up" in a bed in the studio. She's not so sure.

"What about your credibility?" she asks.

"Ah, I shot that down the tubes years ago."

By this time I've got Mike Collins on my side. He tells Meg as long as I don't horse around with it too much it would be fun. It's important that I don't "cross the line." For crying out loud, this show will go from about 12:45 AM to 1:15 AM. Our more conservative viewers will be snoring. Let's do it! Have some fun. It's Wednesday afternoon and we have to make a decision soon. Stay tuned!

Things are about to get zany. With the 6:00 show fast coming, I edit in a flash frame of Maude/Bea Arthur into the Northridge story. It will be the last story in Sports at 6. At 6:00, the IU press conference starts live via satellite in D.C. Andrae Patterson and A.J. Guyton are at the podium. I am taping this live in the Sports office. After Patterson and Guyton talk about having lost three straight NCAA first-round games, I dart back into editing and butt their sound bites together for a :36 piece. I then cover up part of them with file video of Guyton and Patterson playing. We have a special file tape for IU, Purdue, ND, and others so that tape can be quickly found.

I run back into the Sports office about 6:10. An idea pops into my head. I call extension 266. It's AM 960. Producer David Moore answers.

"David," I say, "Bob Knight is about to talk live on the fine the NCAA gave him. I'll hold this phone up to the monitor so the Weekday SportsBeat radio listeners can hear it live." He thinks that's great and tells co-hosts Tom Dennin and John Fineran. Moore runs all their commercials then so they can get Knight on uninterrupted. I hold the phone and watch as Knight takes the podium at 6:15. Mike Stack walks in.

"Here, hold this phone to the monitor," I say.

With our other phone in Sports, I call 6 PM producer John Haferkamp up in the control room booth. "John, I may not be out there for the Sports tease. I want to hear what Knight says and maybe turn around a quick sound bite." John then tells Cindy Ward and Mike Collins through their ear piece that I may not be on set for the tease right before Sports.

I take the phone back from Stack. As Knight sits down, I tell the SportsBeat listeners that this is Bob Knight live. I give the phone back to Stack who holds it there while I listen. Knight doesn't address the fine at first, so I know I won't have time to turn around a quick bite. It's 6:19 and Sports starts in two minutes. I throw my suit jacket on and run out to the set. I tell the floor director the times and outcues for the Patterson/Guyton piece. By adding that, I've gone over my allotted time and don't have time to get the Northridge piece in at the end of Sports. Argh! That had Flash Frame in it so I tell viewers we'll give away the book tomorrow.

Back in the office I send an e-mail to 11 PM producer Jim Pinkerton telling him my main stories at 11 will be Bob Knight on the fine and a special piece on Adams. I then head home where Sherrad has some of my favorite clam chowder piping hot. We sit at the table and talk about her day. She tells me Jack got upset at soccer and left the game. We've got Jack involved in youth sports, but to be honest, I don't think he's going to be superstar sports boy. His main interests are science and building. At five years old, he already wants to be either an architect or a guy who finds dinosaur bones. It wouldn't bother me a bit if he didn't go crazy about sports. I just want him to do what God's will is for him to do. I do want him to be involved in sports to the extent of always exercising and staying in shape, but I'm not going to haul him to all sorts of games and say, "Get interested in this!" Abby looks like she might get into sports. Sherrad was an outstanding sprinter at Elkhart Central, so Abby could have some of her athleticism.

Sherrad can't stay long because she is going downtown. She's thinking about working with the South Bend Press Club to do some acting in their skits for the annual Hoaxes. She takes off and I end up staying with the kids until 8:45. We play Grizzly Bear, where I carry Abby and we chase Jack all over the house. I growl and come oh-so-close to getting Jack and gobbling him up, but he always "gets away."

Around 9 I get back to the office. I look on the computer to see the Mideast Feed rundown. It indicates they'll be sending a piece on Knight at 9:45, so I decide to wait and watch that before editing Knight coverage for 11. I'll incorporate some elements from their piece into excerpts from his press conference.

The 11:00 Sports goes fine. The Knight story leads. I show Pacers/Pistons, then Mike's 1:32 story on Adams. I cover Michigan Madness, Ball State in the NIT, and Notre Dame baseball.

When I get home, I continue to read Acts. I'm beat, though. I would be better served doing this when fresher. Most nights I'm fine, but by Wednesday the toll of the work week starts to hit—especially during a week like this where there's so much to cover.

THURSDAY MARCH 12

Thursday morning is about as tired as I get. The six-and-a-half hours of sleep just isn't enough. That's another reason why I'm looking forward to moving to dayside. My 35-year-old body can't do what it did at 25. I know 35 isn't "old," but I'm not the buzzball of energy I once was. Back in the '80s at WSBT, sometimes I would do the 11:00 Sports, then get up at 4 AM and meet pro fisherman Don Rank to tape a fishing story on the St. Joseph's river in Elkhart. I'd then work through the 11:00 Sports that night and not get tired at all.

Jack asks me to read him his book, *Strange Creatures*. He's taking it to preschool for Show and Share. We laugh at pictures of warty frogfish, goblin sharks, fanfish, and such extinct critters as Naughangosauros and Estommenosuchus. After pronouncing those, I don't think I'll stumble on any words during the sportscast.

At 11:45 I head to Macri's Deli in downtown South Bend. Every Thursday I meet with several men to have lunch. We've all been on Emmaus Walks in the past. We talk about issues that challenge us in our Christian walks. Things like pride, temptation, thought, prayer life, and study of the Holy Scripture. We usually have four to six men in one of the big booths. Most of the men are older than I so I try to soak up the wisdom they share and apply it to my life. The staff at Macri's always give us great service.

We talk until about 1:10, then head our separate ways. I go on to the station because I know there's a lot to line up. As I plop into my office chair, reporter Ed Ernstes ducks in. Ed and I have been working with the Elkhart Fire Department to schedule a charity basketball game. They want to raise money for a Survive Alive House in Elkhart County. It's a mobile building that's used to educate the young and the elderly about fire safety in homes. Ed asks me to meet with him, Meg, and Mike Ivory of the fire department next week. I jot it down on my calendar.

In the mail is a nice note from Angela Overmyer and the eighth grade staff at Grissom School. She thanks WSBT for our recent charity game there. It ended up raising nearly $1,500 for their Washington, D.C., trip in May. I appreciate the card, but Grissom deserves most of the credit for the big crowd that night. The parents really support the kids.

I pop into Meg's office. She has the resume tape of Donna Fendrick. She's the candidate for our 11:00 sports anchor job. I take the beta tape back into one of our edit booths and glance at her paper resume. She's currently the weekend sports anchor at WMTV-TV in Portland, Maine. She writes that on the tape she has two anchor segments (from December 6 and February 22) and three different clips of her doing live reports from the field. She also includes two feature stories she put together. As I watch her anchoring, I'm impressed. She handles highlights well and shows wit. While describing the Tennessee/Auburn game she says, "Peyton Manning to Marcus Nash! The N-A-S-H D-A-S-H begins!!"

After viewing a few minutes of her anchoring, I fast forward to her live shots. She looks very poised in the field. There's a lot of clips of her at local basketball games, which relieves me. I was concerned there was too much national content in her anchoring segments. One of her feature packages is a wonderfully crafted story on a young girl with one leg who is an outstanding skier. Her other one is on her dreaming of becoming a pro baseball player. It's great! She comes across like Madonna in *A League of Their Own*. I zip back into Meg's office.

"Let's hire her," I say. "I think she's great."

Meg and Tim are enthused also. They still worry there might be some reluctance from some viewers to accept a female sports anchor in this market. It baffles me that some viewers could not handle someone as qualified as her. Having grown up with a mother who was extremely successful as a professor and author, I never have understood some of society's problem with women achieving professional success in any endeavor. Meg tells me she will look through Donna's whole tape that afternoon. We then talk about the Friday night "Hoop It Up" show. They tell me they don't want me to host it in a bed. Darn! One of their main concerns is that a bed couldn't be lit properly in the short time we have until Friday night. There also might be some viewers are offended although I doubt "67-year-old Margaret of Mentone, Indiana" will be up watching. I respect their decision and move on.

As I get back in Sports, Ring! It's Luis Caban of Plymouth. We're playing a charity game there Monday night to raise money for the Migrant Program at Plymouth High School. These particular students don't speak English well. The game is raising money so they can go to see the museums in Chicago. Luis is concerned the awful weather has hurt ticket sales. I tell him I'll do Sports live down there Monday at 5 and 6 to try to get a good walk-up crowd.

On the computer, I get an angry e-mail. I recently ran a Gene Keady interview clip on the 11:00 Sports. Upstairs, the person who types in the name of the interview accidentally put an IU logo next to Keady's name. It appeared on air for two seconds before the director realized the mistake and quickly took it off air. This person who wrote the e-mail is a Purdue fan and is ticked off about it. I would e-mail them back, but I keep forgetting how to respond to viewer e-mail.

Bethel College is playing in the NAIA Tourney out in Idaho this afternoon. The game is on 1270 AM radio. Oddly enough, because of our location downtown and our big, thick walls, I can't get the station on the radio in the Sports office. I head out to the parking lot, get in my car, and drive down in front of the station. I sit there with the engine idling and listen to the broadcast so I can give a score in the 5:00 TV sportscast. WSBT employees leaving for the day give me strange looks as they exit the building. I do look sort of odd sitting by myself in my car right in front of the building. At 5:15 the first half ends, so I go back in the building and do the 5:00 Sports. Little do the viewers know what all I went through to give them a halftime score of Bethel-Southwestern (KS).

At 6:05 I tromp back out to my car. As I sit there, regular citizens walk by me on the sidewalk and do a doubletake. I can just hear them saying, "Isn't that Charlie Adams sitting by himself in a car?" Eventually I turn off the engine and just listen to the radio while sitting in my big parka coat. I look like somebody who is despondent. I think I'll charge the station for gasoline used while idling in a vehicle pursuing a sports score. Ken Biggins in Accounting would do a double take if he saw that.

The announcer keeps saying, "Bethel is up by 14 points." I have to have a SCORE before I can go back in. The game finally ends at 6:15 with Bethel winning 100-84. I sprint back in the building and call the guys down on SportsBeat before dashing in to do the TV sports. The Flash Frame at 6 pops up during a piece on Northridge gearing up for the Plymouth Regional. It's Bea Arthur, better know as Maude. Actually, this Flash Frame comes from the Golden Girls, so Jim Pinkerton was briefed earlier that "Maude, Bea Arthur, or Golden Girls" would be accepted as a winning guess. Gloria Baker of South Bend is the first caller to get through who knew it was Bea Arthur. After the news I call up Gloria. "I figured out who it was because of her hair," says Gloria. "That's how I guessed who it was. Her hair!" She wins a free copy of *Pioneers of the Hardwood.* Sensing that she may not have a voracious desire to read about the Fort Wayne Zollnar Pistons I suggest she might want to give it as a gift to a grandparent or something like that.

I head home to chase the kids around and spend time with Sherrad. She and I are both fighting colds so earlier I called her to suggest she not worry about making something. I end up heating up some spaghetti.

Back at the station I start outlining the Friday night show. Purdue-Delaware will lead since we're coming right out of CBS' NCAA coverage. Homer and Bryce Drew postgame interviews from the Valpo-Mississippi game will be next. Then Bethel in Idaho. The Notre Dame women vs. Southwest Missouri State in the NCAA's. The Regional games will come next starting with 4-A and going to 1-A. The next challenge is determining how much time each game gets in the show so that the show times out to 25 minutes of actual airtime. We don't want to be "light" where I finish with all the content of our show and there's still two minutes left to fill. In that case we could roll credits of all WSBT employees or re-rack one of the highlight tapes and play music under it to finish out the show. On the other hand, we don't want to be heavy where I have to drop one or two of the tapes from the show at the end.

Tonight's 11:00 Sports is pretty basic. I'll lead with Indiana-Oklahoma. With IU up 19, I go ahead and put together the morning sports TV wrap. I edit together a bunch of IU highlights and then narrate them. I end it by saying, "IU rolls on to an easy win over Oklahoma." I e-mail the morning producers to insert the final score at that point. I then leave the tape on their desk.

Oh oh.

Indiana blows the 19-point lead. Oklahoma sends the game to overtime. Two things result because of this. Producer Jim Pinkerton now wants me to be on the set at the start of the 11:00 News to do a story on the suddenly dramatic game. Also, I'm going to have to totally re-do the morning wrap. Because IU has frittered away the lead, I call CBS in New York to get the satellite coordinates for the postgame interview. Knight should have some interesting comments. They tell me it will be on SBS 6/Transponder 2, KU band.

IU ends up winning in overtime. The game ends at 10:15. I go back into the main editing room and watch the satellite feed. It shows a live picture of the NCAA interview room. At 10:30 Knight comes in and analyzes the game. Once he's talked for 10 minutes, I yank out the tape and head to an edit booth. In five minutes I put together a :58 piece for the lead story of the News. I give it to Jim Pinkerton and tell him to tell the director I'll ad lib the intro on the set.

Now I "regret" having sent Stack home early. He's an IU alum so I wanted him to be able to watch the game with friends because the Hoosiers are a big deal to him. Now I could use the help, but it's no big deal. I get the morning wrap back and recut it to where it reflects the "changed nature" of a game I assumed would be an IU blowout.

At 10:59 I go out on the set with Mike and Cindy and throw to the piece I put together. At 11:02 I leave the set and head back into editing to put together Bulls-Mavericks highlights. The theme of this night is "Charlie assumes wrong." I assume the Bulls blow out the pitiful Mavs so I cut a bunch of Bulls highlights. Five minutes later my jaw drops as the wire says Dallas wins in overtime. There's no time to change the highlights to show key Maverick buckets, so I move on to getting the Michigan District scores. Some are on the wire. Others have been phoned in. I call the *Kalamazoo Gazette* to get some and then the *South Bend Tribune*. They are always gracious enough to help me out even though they don't have to.

A story has moved on the wire. It's about Alonzo Spellman's bizarre behavior in Chicago this whole week. It indicates he's now being treated for depression and talking of suicide. I pray he doesn't entertain those thoughts. It makes me think of part of Ken Davis' book I've been reading the past week. In a chapter on "The Penalty of Sin," Davis writes of a man named Jim who kills himself.

> *The note Jim left on the motel dresser was the only thing left behind by this once vital, potential-filled life. How the demons in hell must have leaned forward in anticipation as Jim wrote! And when he pulled the trigger, they undoubtedly jumped to their feet, cheering wildly as Satan threw back his head and laughed. This time he had destroyed not just his victim's self-confidence but his very life. It is Satan's ultimate victory.*

Spellman has been upset the Bears are thinking about trading him. I'm sure there are other things tearing him up as well. Mike Singletary, who is a Christian, is counseling him, so I feel good that Alonzo is listening to him. Singletary has got a book coming out (that will be out when you read this) called *Daddy's Home at Last*. From what I understand, it's a wonderful book on priorities for husbands and fathers.

I head out to the studio and fire through the sportscast. I then navigate the icy patches outside the station to get to my car and go home. Since I did my "Bethel radio listening" earlier in the day, I don't have to go far. The car is parked right in front of the building.

FRIDAY MARCH 13

I spend the morning playing with the kids and running errands for Sherrad. At 12:20 I flip on the TV at home to WSBT for the NCAA Tourney first-round game between Valparaiso and Mississippi. My alma mater is Mississippi. I'm wound up for them, but I also pull for Valpo. Their classy coach Homer Drew is a tremendous Christian role model. Their star player Bryce is also a highly visible Christian who exemplifies the qualities America would like to see in young people. The game is close and intense. At halftime, I zip down to the station to catch the second half there while getting set for a very challenging Friday of sports coverage.

On Fridays I take in my dirty dress shirts. WSBT has a deal with Ziker Cleaning where the anchors' stuff their shirts and other on-air clothes into a Ziker's bag and drop it off in a small room at the station. It's something of a dressing room. There's a whole bunch of ties in there that Luke and I share. An observant viewer would notice over the course of a week that Luke might wear a particular tie on Tuesday and I might end up taking it off the rack and wearing it Friday.

In the Sports office, with the Valpo game on, I check voice mail. Armando Femia's mother wants a VHS copy of the Athlete of the Week story. Argh! We are not allowed to make copies for viewers (unless the station is subpoenaed in some court case). We get tons of calls from viewers wanting copies of stories that aired. A typical call goes like this:

VIEWER: "Charlie, I wasn't up last night but a neighbor called and said there was a shot of my nephew Buster on your Sports. He was at the Riley game."

CHARLIE: "Okay. I guess that was a cutaway shot (cutaway shots are generally two second shots of fans in the stands). I really would love to help you but I'm not allowed to make copies. We have to take it upstairs to get it dubbed over. As many requests as we get, it's just impossible."

VIEWER: "Well, could I pay you for it?"

CHARLIE: (At this point in some cases I could ask for $100 and probably get it, but obviously I don't) "No. I'm sorry."

The viewer has one of these two replies:

VIEWER: "Harumph! I don't see why you can't."

VIEWER: "I understand. Still, I just wanted to see if it was possible."

The next voice mail is from Patti Hostetler. She is WSBT President and General Manager Jim Freeman's secretary and, in many ways, the heart and soul of the station. Mike Collins recently told me just how much she does for WSBT and how much she loves the place. She tells me the brand new uniform tops are in for the WSBT charity basketball team. I recently approached her to replace our old double knit ones. I had lugged them around in a suitcase to game sights for years. Sometimes I would forget to wash them after games and they would sit in that suitcase in the back of my car fermenting for months.

As Valpo and Mississippi go back and forth, 6:00 producer John Haferkamp walks in the office. "We've sent Ray Roth over to LaPorte today to do a community story on the people getting ready for tonight's Regional Championship," John says. "We want you on the set in the first block of the News to introduce it." No problem, I respond.

Ring! A man calls and identifies himself as a Valparaiso alum. Get a load of this conversation.

VALPO ALUM: "Charlie, I'm stuck in the office at work. Is the Valpo game on any radio station in South Bend?"

CHARLIE: "Not that I know of. It's on WSBT-TV right now. Just turn it on."

VALPO ALUM: "I can't. I'm at work. My boss frowns on that."

CHARLIE: "There's four minutes to go. Surely your boss would let you go to the coffee break room and watch it. This is the biggest game in school history!"

VALPO ALUM: "I just can't…"

That's one of the problems with today's fast-paced, ultra competitive society. Bosses keep their poor workers to the grindstone. We are losing sight of special events. Come on! Let a guy break away to watch a very special game in the history of his particular university. Just last night I let Mike Stack off early so he could watch IU at home. Before hanging up, I tell the exasperated fella to keep calling our newsroom for frequent updates. I hope his boss doesn't catch him on the phone or surely the employee will be beaten senseless by a two by four.

Back to reality. It's 2:15 and I head to the newsroom to watch the game's final frantic moments. Everyone in there knows I'm a Mississippi alum. To downplay a potential loss, I carry on like the game is not THAT big a deal to me. "Actually, I'm more of an Ole Miss football fan," I say. That's a total fib. I like both teams equally, but I just don't want to get kidded relentlessly should Ole Miss lose.

Sure enough. Bryce Drew nails a three-pointer at the buzzer to win the game. A dagger through my heart would have been less painful. It is an incredible finish, though, and I do feel good for Homer and

Bryce. Admittedly, I conjure up images of them tied to a train track as the Ole Miss coach has them in the train's sights, but that thought is kept to myself.

Everyone in the newsroom is stunned by the excitement of the shot. Everyone, even non-sports fans, is entralled by the endless series of slow motion replays by CBS of the big shot. As I trudge back into the Sports office, there's a viewer e-mail waiting for me. It's from a Western Michigan fan. Their team has been playing Clemson at the same time WSBT has carried the Valpo game. The e-mail reads: "It would have been nice to see the last 17 seconds of the Western Michigan game while the Valpo game was in timeout with 40 seconds to go!"

Ring! A Kentucky fan calls and gets angry at me for WSBT not carrying the Kentucky-South Carolina State game.

There's always a collection of folks in our tiny Sports office or at the doorway. There are constant discussions going on about everything from Notre Dame football to what's happening that moment in sports. I share with everyone my "theory" on the Bryce Drew shot. "I really think God was involved it it." That draws scoffs from one guy, who paraphrases Bob Knight's quote. He says Knight one time said God had better things to do than get involved with sports. Another naysayer says, "If God cared about Valpo, what about the losing team?" I nod and listen to these comebacks.

"Hear me out," I say. "In 1994 Bryce was on the Valparaiso High basketball team that had Clay all but beat. They blew the lead and lost in overtime. That had to be awful for Bryce. To be *that* close and then have the most prestigious championship in all of high school athletics slip away. Well, he handled himself in a first-class manner in defeat. He went on to do the loving thing by playing for his father at Valpo even though he could have signed with bigger programs and won all sorts of NCAA Tourney games. I really think God blessed him in this game with that shot."

Hey! It's my feeling. I may be wrong or right. I do know that shortly after "the shot," Bryce says that he feels an angel lifted the ball above the rim. When it was released, Homer felt it was going to be short.

The phone rings in Sports. It's Jeff of CBS Sports in New York. He wants to know if we can get a crew to Valparaiso to get reaction from fans on Drew's shot. CBS wants to use that over the weekend. They are going to milk this shot for everything they can get. I transfer the call to News to see if they can send someone.

My conversations with New York have become terse over the years. When they call, they expect you to drop everything and do what they want. Back in the late '80s and early '90s when Notre Dame Football was highly ranked, they would call all the time looking for specific video. No kidding, this is a call I got one time from a CBS producer. The fella was born and raised in New York City.

"Chaw-leeeee, I'm producing the opening segment of the Notre Dame game. I need some shots of South Bend."

I said okay. I asked what exactly he was looking for.

"How about some shots of tumbleweeds downtown."

He was dead serious. It was like he thought Marshal Matthew Dillon and Festus Hagen lived here. I told him he might be thinking of Kansas and that this was Indiana.

As I start to write the NCAA and Hoosier Hysteria-saturated 5:00 and 6:00 sportscasts, Assignment Editor John Snyder comes into Sports. We talk about my upcoming trip to Augusta National to cover The Masters. He tells me that the station I usually work with out of Spartanburg, South Carolina, has not been getting back to him. He's a little worried. I tell him not to sweat it. I've worked out of their satellite truck the past four years and everything will fall into place.

CBS' NCAA Tournament coverage runs long and spills into our 5:00 newscast. The producer must immediately start dropping stories because we won't go on until about 5:15. News reporter Robert Borrelli is standing by live in Goshen for a big news story. Everyone waits on CBS to sign off. The producer calls me and tells me I'll only have time to get in Bryce Drew's shot and postgame reaction from Homer.

The News does start at 5:15 and they get on a couple of stories and Sam does some weather. At 5:25 Luke and Debra introduce me and I get all excited talking about Bryce's incredible shot. "Watch this," I say.

There's a problem though. Upstairs, the machine that plays on-air tapes has gone goofy. Just before Sports, it starts rewinding the Bryce Drew tape. The tape operator can't stop it. Video gremlins must be in the machine. On the set, floor director Rod Copley starts stretching his arms. That signals me to stretch out my introduction. They're obviously having problems upstairs. I start rambling on like some scatter-brained cat about the game, hoping the tape will come up. I should wear an I.F.B. earpiece for every sportscast. That way the producer in the booth could tell me exactly what's happening, but problems rarely happen so I don't mess with putting that thing in my ear and connecting chords before every sportscast. Plus, I constantly get wax build-up in my ear piece and that's a hassle. Eventually, the director puts the scoreboards up and that's all I do in Sports.

Afterwards, I just shrug my shoulders and go back into the office wondering what happened. In years past I probably would have thrown a fit and stomped around. I've had a problem with getting real angry and popping off with my mouth. It's a bad example for a Christian to give. Since my Emmaus Walk, my prayers have been directed towards reacting better and I am comforted by a peaceful feeling from the Holy Spirit. When I do feel myself getting angry and about to fly into an immature tizzy, I think of these scriptures from Proverbs:

PROVERBS 14:29—"Patient people have great understanding, but people with quick tempers show their foolishness."

PROVERBS 16:32—"Patience is better than strength. Controlling your temper is better than capturing a city."

COLOSSIANS 3:8 gets right to the point—"But now also put these things out of your life: anger, bad temper, doing or saying things to hurt others, and using evil words when you talk." The only time I turn the air blue is when something goes wrong at work. But again, through prayer I've come a long way in these areas.

The producer tells me what happened and I understand. Those things happen every blue moon. Knowing that I am going to head to Plymouth for the 3-A Regional championship game right after our 6:00 sportscast, I call Tom's Restaurant to pick up a club sandwich. They're right across the street from WSBT. My plan is to go pick up the sandwich and sit in the car listening to the Bethel game again. What a sight I'll be. People will think something's wrong with me—sitting in my car in front of the station by myself eating. Instead, I see Mike Stack as he gets set to head to Michigan City to cover the Adams-LaPorte game. I tell Mike to listen to the Bethel game on 1270 AM and call the newsroom with the final.

The 6:00 sportscast goes well. It's saturated with NCAA coverage and a soundbite from Brian Wray of Plymouth talking about the Northridge game.

Photographer Brian O'Donnell and I get in a news vehicle and drive to Plymouth right after the News. Most weeks I get out in the field more than I have this one. Because of so many "administrative" decisions this week, I've been in the office more than I like. It feels great tonight to get out to a gamesite.

The atmosphere at Plymouth is vibrant. The gym is jam packed. A sea of green represents the Northridge fans. The Plymouth faithful are decked out in fire engine red. As I walk in I get the usual comments, "You look different in person than you do on TV," and "I didn't know you were that tall."

Actually, I love going to Plymouth. The people there are so warm and friendly. I dubbed the gym "Ray Roth Arena" years ago because our veteran news reporter lives in Plymouth. One of these days they'll probably really name the gym and that will be it for "Ray Roth Arena." Hopefully, they will name a locker room after Ray then.

The noise level is thunderous during the game. I stand by the corner of the bleachers jotting down notes on my pad. If a player makes a really nice play, I'll put down two stars next to my note on it. That tells me to definitely use that highlight. Brian Wray of Plymouth nails three three-pointers in the first half. Plymouth goes up 24-10.

At halftime something happens as it does in just about every public bathroom I use. Just as I get done relieving myself, some guy ambles up and says, "Hey, Charlie Adams! Good to see ya!" He then shakes my hand vigorously and proceeds to carry on about how he can't stand Warsaw.

Northridge makes a gutty comeback in the second half, but the Pilgrims go on to win. Afterwards, I interview Coach Jack Edison of Plymouth and Coach Steve Austin of Northridge. I also talk to Wray. I ask him what it's like winning a Regional Championship in *Class* Basketball. "It still feels great," the state's leading scorer says. "A Regional Championship is a Regional Championship."

Ray Roth is still anti-class basketball. Before the State Tournament, he had proclaimed to me he was boycotting all tournament games. But with Plymouth having such a fine team, sure enough, Ray showed up to watch the Sectional Championship game against Washington.

"But I didn't pay to get in," Ray told me earlier in the week. "I got a buddy to let me in. That's how I'll continue my protest. I won't financially support the tournament."

On this night against Northridge, Ray also got his buddy at the door to let him slide in. "The semi-boycott continues," Rays says.

Dozens of children surround the Plymouth players to get autographs. One kid comes up to me and hands me a program to sign. "You're on TV aren't you,?" he blurts out.

A few minutes later some ladies strike up a conversation with me. One offers this observation: "Ever since you came back to WSBT (in 1993), you've been more dignified than when you were here before." I don't quite know what to say to that one.

On the 30-minute trip back to South Bend, Brian and I listen to WSBT NewsTalk 960 as Rick Carter and Bob Berger broadcast the exciting Adams-LaPorte game. At one point, Rick describes a basket as a "bunny."

"What's a bunny?' Brian asks.

"It's a layup," I respond. "Usually old people call them bunnies. My Dad does. Actually, Dad also calls layups 'crip shots' sometimes too. That's what they called them back then. I have no idea why Rick is calling layups bunnies. He's only 39."

Brian and I get back to the WSBT Empire around 10:00. The best we can figure, CBS' NCAA Tournament coverage will end between 12:30 AM and 1:00 AM. That's when our 30-minute live "Hoop It Up" show will start.

I work with Producer Jim Pinkerton to fine tune the run-down in the computer. I rewrite some lead-ins to stories. I then go back into the main editing room and give editor Tom Nicholl some insight as to how to edit the Notre Dame women's highlights. Since we have a whopping 30-minute show, each game gets a ton of coverage. I end up putting together a three-minute story on the Plymouth-Northridge game. That's great because it gives the game comprehensive coverage. When done with that, I scan through Gene Keady's postgame interview of the Boilers' rout of the Delaware Blue Hens and edit a sound bite where he talks about Jaraan Cornell's return (Jaraan is my favorite college basketball player—he is so unselfish).

Around 12:20, everybody is about done with their responsibilities. I still haven't sorted scripts the way I like. I haven't viewed the Bremen-Boone Grove tape. But WHAM! CBS puts up credits like they are going off the air. Oh geez. The director and producers sprint upstairs. I run out on to the set and put on my microphone. Somebody runs into an edit booth to tell Mike Stack he'd better finish the Adams-LaPorte story fast.

False alarm. CBS goes to commercial, then comes back and fills until 12:30 with on-set analysis. I catch a deep breath, get my scripts in order, and wait for our show to start. It flows wonderfully. I'm genuinely touched by the enthusiasm of small schools like Kouts (1-A) and Bremen (2-A) that have won Regionals for the first time ever. I regret we didn't have anyone over towards Fort Wayne for Bethany Christian's Regional title. Just mentioning the score is a letdown.

The "Hoop It Up" show ends about 1:00 AM. Afterwards, I thank all the photographers for the great job they did in getting highlights and postgame interviews. These Friday night shows are a wonderful example of teamwork and I'm proud to be associated with everyone that works on them.

SATURDAY MARCH 14

Late in the morning, Sherrad and the kids and I head to Pinnacle for a workout. Inevitably, someone will strike up a sports conversation in the locker room with me. Not that I mind at all. I enjoy hearing viewers' opinions of sports. I helps me determine what they want to see covered in many cases. As I take off my jacket and put on my exercise clothes, a man about 35 tells me he really enjoys reading columnist/ sportswriter David Haugh in the *South Bend Tribune*. "He writes with integrity," the man says. "I think he's extremely talented. I could see him writing for *Sports Illustrated*." The man also asks me if I think Bryce Drew will play in the NBA. "He'll be a first-round draft pick," I respond. That surprises him somewhat. "He's a lock because of his talent. Plus, the NBA needs players with his character. There's so many ding dongs in that league."

In the evening, Sherrad and I go to the southside home of Terry and Lissa Newton for our monthly Euchre League. Having played this card game only about six times, my ability is at the bonehead level. Everyone else has played for years and knows all the subtle strategies.

I just try to hang in there and not mess up my partner too much. I'm so bad that I'm given "pull back" privileges. Whenever I toss down the wrong card, everyone at the table takes pity on me by allowing me to "pull the card back" and put down another. Also playing are former Texas High School football great Randy Brooks and his wife Janet, Mark and Jean Rutledge, Larry and Karen Hildebrandt, and Bob and Angie Lingenfelter. To give you an idea of the level of competition, Bob was a college champion in Euchre. He should be in some kind of Euchre Pro League, shouldn't he? He should be captain of the South Bend Bowers or something. To be even semi-competent at Euchre, I need to utilize all my mental capacities. On this night, that's not possible as the TV has the Indiana-Connecticut game on. At each card table (we shift around) I angle for the chair with the best view of what is a very good game. As A.J. Guyton scores, someone says, "Charlie, your turn."

"Huh? Oh. Pass!"

"Spades has already been determined, Charlie."

"Oh, yeah, of course!" I plop down one of my cards that is a heart.

"Now, Charlie, you know if you have a spade you have to play it?"

"I know THAT!"

Euchre goes nonstop for four hours. Everyone keeps their point totals as the winner gets some sort of gift certificate. It usually comes down to two people near the end of the night. Inevitably, one of them will get me as their partner for the last game. You should see the look on their face when they see ol' Charlie sit down. There go their chances.

SUNDAY MARCH 15

Mike Jacob's Sunday School class centers on the theme of "Whatever happened to going to Grandma's House after church for Sunday lunch?" Jo Myers makes an interesting point. She's a grandmother with a potful of grandkids. She says in today's hi-tech world of computers and gadgets, Grandma's house is now boring for the kids. It doesn't have all that stuff. She says she has to visit her grandkids if she wants to visit them.

The discussion heads towards inviting others to your home for fellowship and socializing. It's brought up that's there's a difference between hospitality and entertaining. A lot of people get all worked up when visitors are coming and make sure every shag in the carpet is straight. When the visitors/friends are in their home they hardly have any kind of meaningful talk with them because, as super host, they're running around making sure the food is just right.

Seeing as how my increased Bible reading in the last year has made me Mr. Bible Scholar, I bring up the story in the Bible of Jesus at the home of Martha and Mary. Luke 10:38-42 goes: "As Jesus and his disciples were on their way, he came to a village where a woman named Martha opened her home to him. She had a sister called Mary, who sat at the Lord's feet listening to what he said. But Martha was distracted by all the preparations that had to be made. She came to him and asked, 'Lord, don't you care that my sister has left me to do the work by myself? Tell her to help me!"

"Martha, Martha," the Lord answered, "you are worried and upset about many things, but only this one is needed. Mary has chosen what is better, and it will not be taken away from her." During 45 minutes of round table discussion, I'm surprised that Don Tarner hasn't fired off his strong beliefs. Don tells it like it is. Turns out, he's been snoozing quietly. But, when someone mentions watching TV, he perks up. That's a hot button with Don. He has some passionate feelings about some of the garbage on TV. He's right. A lot of that Hollywood mess will shape you if you watch it too long.

The 11:00 worship service features another fine sermon by Pastor Ed. I've been especially busy lately. It's been two months since my Emmaus Walk. What he says about prayer hits me. "We get up, we're on the clock. We're too busy during the day and then at the end of the day we're too tired to pray—tomorrow, God."

He tells the story of one fella who got "too busy" to pray regularly after he went into business. After a while, his life started going down hill in areas. Then he said, "Lord, I've got so much work to do today. I've got to start it first with you."

As the sermon ends near noon, I notice an odd background noise. Pastor Ed wears a wireless microphone. It turns out because of some bizarre frequency overlap, CBS' coverage of the NCAA Tourney has bled into his microphone. So as Pastor Ed hammers home the conclusion, we can hear CBS' Greg Gumbel in the New York studio sizing up the Duke-Oklahoma State game. During the closing prayer Pastor Ed can't have poignant pauses because "Duke will look to Trajan Langdon to hit the perimeter jump shots" will pipe throughout the church. So he gives it the 77 RPM prayer as his close.

In Disciple Sunday evening, we talk about many things including Ephesians. I find chapters four and five to have so much "insight" from Luke on how we should live. I really wished I had hammered this home more as a young adult. You've got to have that spiritual armor before you go out into the "world" as a young person.

Part Three
March 16-May 17, 1998

MARCH
Monday
16

Pull Up Your Pants

An early morning conference call with the station starts the day. News Director Meg Sauer and Executive Producer Tim Ceravolo give me a ring at home. With Purdue and Valparaiso going to the Sweet 16 in St. Louis, they want me to go to the Gateway City to cover it. They propose that satellite truck operator Wilson Johnson leave Wednesday and drive to St. Louis. Mike Stack and I would fly down Thursday to start doing coverage. Our concern is staffing coverage of Hoosier Hysteria on Saturday. With class basketball, our local teams are spaced all over Indiana. Plymouth is going to Muncie. Bremen's in Fort Wayne. Elkhart Central and LaPorte are in West Lafayette. Bethany Christian's in Marion. We discuss options for 30 minutes.

Upon arrival to the station around 1:00, the Notre Dame Sports Information Department calls to say the women's basketball team is flying in at 2:30. Last night they stunned national power Texas Tech, 74-59, in Lubbock to move to the Sweet 16. I decide to swing by Corporate Wings after taping a "Making a Difference" feature. Photographer Laurent and I leave WSBT at 1:15 to tape "Making a Difference." Since Laurent is from France, I have to drive the station vehicle. I suppose it's because he doesn't have a driver's license. We pull up to "The Patch" on West Washington. On the door leading into the business is a small sign reading: If you're pants are hanging down, don't come in! Inside, Mrs. Adeline tells me the sign is all about respect. The business owner was tired of youngsters wearing those loose pants "where you could see their butts." If they wanted their hair cut in her place, they'd better get rid of those ridiculous baggy pants that make boys look like babies in diapers.

Invigorated by her strong feelings on respect, Laurent and I zip over to Corporate Wings. A bunch of folks from The Fast Break Club are waiting for Muffet's incredible Irish. The Fast Break Club is the booster group of the women's basketball team. In the lobby, I interview them about Notre Dame's shocking win at Texas Tech. Keep in mind, there were 8,000 fans jammed in the building last night—95% of them were rooting AGAINST Notre Dame and FOR Texas Tech. The key for the Irish was 6' 5" freshman center Ruth Riley. Plagued by first-half foul trouble, she broke loose for all of her 23 points in the second half. Fast Break Club members have made colorful signs declaring "You Can't Stop the Ruth!"

I interview Muffet right after the team plane lands. She is one of my favorite coaches to cover. For starters, she is an excellent interview. Her answers are energetic, informative, and clearly stated. She's a super nice person who can flat out coach the game and run a program. Speaking of Notre Dame women's basketball, in all my years at WSBT, the most impressive accomplishment of ANY sports team I have covered was the 1996-97 Notre Dame women's basketball team reaching The Final Four. Most fans don't have any idea how hard it is to reach the Women's Final Four. It is much, much harder than the men's tourney, primarily because women's teams still have to win some games on a powerful opponent's home court. In '97, Muffet's Irish had to beat Texas in Austin before 10,000 screaming Longhorn fans.

The evening is highlighted by a trip to Plymouth for a benefit basketball team game. The WSBT All-Stars are playing faculty from Plymouth High School. Money raised is going to the Plymouth Migrant Program. I bring five autographed WSBT coffee cups down and sell them for $10 each. That money goes into their kitty. Luis Caban is the man who did a lot of hard work setting up this benefit game. Catherine Redden is the Migrant Program teacher at Plymouth.

The game sets back the sport of basketball 10 years. Veteran reporter Ray "Mr. Plymouth" Roth joins us for this game. Ray's conditioning is not exactly where we would incorporate him in a full-court press.

Two trips up and down the court and Ray heads for the pine. We end up getting dusted in the game. Folks from Plymouth start dribbling a basketball as the Doctor delivers them. Coach Jack Edison is in all delivery rooms to (a) encourage the newborns to establish their fundamentals and realize the importance of good, hard defense, and (b) tell them that Warsaw is to be dreaded. The teachers from Plymouth run down-screens on us and fill the lanes on their fast break. They block out and fire crisp outlet passes.

Upon getting back, I get a call from former WSBT producer Dean Turcol. He tells me he's coming up in April for highly respected sportscaster Dean Huppert's wedding. Turcol's now in Orlando where he handles publicity for the Budweiser Water Ski team.

One time when Dean was a producer at WSBT, he was in the control booth upstairs producing the station's important live election coverage. He had his hands full, to say the least. Dean would get all hyper on big nights like this and did not like distractions. Since the station hires a lot of extra workers to staff election night, they provided a whole bunch of boxes of Kentucky Fried Chicken in a room downstairs. These people were new to WSBT. I went in the room with the chicken and put a sign up that said: "Please pay just $2 for the chicken. Please take your money to Dean Turcol upstairs in the producer's booth." A steady stream of folks kept going into Dean's booth during the night handing him $2 bills and asking him where they could purchase beverages to wash down the tasty chicken. "Are you Dean Turcol?" they would ask politely. "YES. YES I AM. WHO ARE YOU? WHAT IS THIS MONEY FOR? CAN'T YOU SEE I'M BUSY! THIS IS LIVE COVERAGE!!" Finally, he got on the station intercom and told people to quit coming upstairs!

MARCH
Thurs.-Fri.
19-20

Covering the NCAA Tournament

This is going to be a looooooong day. Photographer Rick Stuckey, Mike Stack, and I are flying to St. Louis to cover Purdue and Valpo in the NCAA's. We've got a 7:30 AM flight out of South Bend, so I get to WSBT around 5:45 to do a little office work before we head to Michiana Regional Airport. As I zombie-walk down the hallway yawning, Jack Reichert's voice blares out over the station public address system. "Hey, Charlie, come on in the studio!" I whirl around and dutifully walk into the vibrant Sunny 101.5 FM studio, which is right down the hall from the WSBT-TV newsroom.

I spend a few fun-filled minutes talking with Jack, Shannon, Bruce Kayser, and their listening audience about our upcoming trip. It's remarkable how peppy, perky, bright, and alert they are at that hour. Their wit is razor sharp. Jack, Shannon, and Bruce are a wonderful team to listen to in the morning. In person, they are just as nice as they come across on the airwaves. They've got a hilarious CD out that includes the best of their work—including their "Happy Birthday calls. All sales from the CD benefit the Boys and Girls Club. You can get it at the WSBT-TV front desk, Sachet Sue's at Scottsdale Mall, Jordan Ford, Monteith Tire, and AfDent Dental. They ask for minimum $5 donation but many folks give more because of the cause. The CD is called "A Taste of the Sunny

101.5 Morning Show with Jack, Shannon and Bruce." In the past when I took our boy Jack to preschool I would almost have to pull off the side of the road because I would laugh so hard at their morning "birthday" calls.

Jack Reichert is a well known Washington Panther fan. He gets so wound up whenever Washington plays arch rival LaSalle that boils develop on his upper thighs and lower back area.

At the airport, I get my seat switched to an exit row. At 6' 5," I am miserable flying commercial airplanes unless I can get on the exit row. It has more space for your legs because the exit door is right there. The stewardress lets us "exit row folks" know that having an extra 10 inches or so of leg space does come with responsibility. In the event of an an emergency we will need to help the passengers exit. In other words, we get to be stomped on as they madly plunge out the exit door. It's one delay after another on the plane. Blame the fog. For some reason, we fly to Detroit before going to St. Louis. Isn't that going the wrong direction? We always do that. When Notre Dame played Navy in Dublin, Ireland, we flew to Belgium and then back to Ireland.

There are more delays in Detroit. After leaving South Bend at 7:30 AM we get to St. Louis at 3:00 PM. We could have ridden on Bessie the Mule and made it faster! There's no time to check into the Airport Marriott because we are doing live shots for the 5:00 and 6:00 News. We get our rental car and drive downtown to the Kiel Center, home of the St. Louis Blues and sight of the Midwest Regionals. After the obligatory four to five wrong turns (Rick was reading the map: "Uh, you need to take a right turn... at that last exit we just passed!") we pull into the parking lot of the Kiel Center. The WSBT satellite truck is parked there. Engineer Wilson Johnson has got it all revved up and ready to go. Now *all* we need to do is quickly shoot some video, do some interviews, and edit it all in time to feed back to WSBT via satellite at 4:50 PM. We've brought two cameras.

Standing across the street from the arena, I lay out the battleplan. "We don't have much time. Mike, you go on your own. Find a feature, an angle of some kind. Shoot it so you can edit it fast. Let's go!" Mike hustles across the street and disappears into the arena. Rick and I go in a different door. Thankfully, Purdue's practice is still going on. On the way in, we spot some Valparaiso fans and interview them. That will work for our segment early in the 5:00 News. Alongside the court, Rick sprays Purdue's practice. No, he does not unleash a garden hose on them. "Spraying" is TV News terminology for quickly getting a variety of video shots. Their practice ends at 4:30. We grab a quick interview with Boilermaker sophomore Jaraan Cornell of South Bend and then hustle back across the street to the satellite truck. Rick immediately begins setting up his camera for the live shot. He connects cables from the satellite truck to his camera. I dart inside the truck and sit down at the editing machine. It's 4:35. I have no time to "write" a story. Based on years of experience, I know exactly what I can put together in this time frame of about 12 minutes. I will butt together the sound bites of the Valpo fans, then voice track a narration of Purdue's practice. That will lead into a sound bite with Jaraan Cornell. The only video I'll have to cover is Purdue's practice. With my hands operating the editor in whirlwind fashion, I crank out a 1:10 piece on Purdue's practice and the Valpo fans. I get done at 4:45. During this time, Wilson is getting the satellite dish pointed in the correct position. We've been given coordinates to align to and Wilson lines them all up. He calls the Satellite Access Center and gains permission to access the transponder we've requested.

When you buy satellite time, you get it in increments of 5, 10, 15, or however minutes. If we order, say, a 10-minute window, we have to have fed our stuff by the time it ends or we barge into another station's satellite window. They then get mad and start hollering to Satellite Access Center, so it can get pretty wild in crunch time if everyone's not in sync.

At 4:50, WSBT editor Judy "Purdue fan" Peters is on the phone with us. We play the tape in St. Louis and via satellite Judy records it in South Bend. Within minutes it is upstairs and ready to be aired at 5:04.

Here comes the really fun part. The NCAA makes all TV reporters do their "live" shots outside the arena. That's swell if it's a decent day. Unfortunately, the weather in St. Louis is terrible. It's sleeting and raining and doing all sorts of yucky weather stuff. But there I am, standing there like a ding dong. I'm sure some viewers at home go, "Why doesn't he show some common sense and get indoors." I connect my earpiece do an I.F.B. box that Rick gives me. That allows there to be communication between the producer in the booth at WSBT and me. As the 5:00 News starts, I talk with producer Jerry Siefring through my microphone and listen to him in my earpiece. "What's your roll cue, Charlie?" Jerry asks.

A roll cue is what I say that indicates to the director when to roll the tape. "I don't know. It will be obvious. Something like, 'Valpo fans are fired up about the Sweet Sixteen.'"

It's 5:02. Jerry indicates there are two more stories before they come to me. During this whole time, Mike Stack has come back to the satellite truck and is hastily putting together a piece for the 6:00 News.

At 5:04, anchors Luke Choate and Debra Daniel toss to me in St. Louis. I can hear them but can't see them. I cheerfully introduce my report while fending off sleet with the satellite truck umbrella Wilson has given me. When done, I tell the viewers that I'll be back in Sports and again at 6. When the segment ends, I hightail it back to the warm satellite truck. "What are you putting together?" I ask Mike as I warm my hands in the truck. Seeing this, Wilson digs up some gloves for me. Wilson is a great guy to work with on these trips. Mike informs me he's doing a piece on St. Louis citizens getting wound up for the Regionals and how the fans have really taken to Valpo. Every hat and shirt with Valpo on it sold out during the practice sessions today. I grab the phone and call Matt Burridge in the Sports office at WSBT. "What have you cut for 5 Sports?" I ask Matt. "I recorded Homer Drew's and Gene Keady's press conferences off the bird (satellite feed)," Matt says. "I've put together a 24-second bite on Keady for 5 that you can throw to."

By this time of the day I'm pretty tired from the travel and the deadline pressure. That means I'm prime material for a temper fit. I get on the phone with one of the newsroom decision makers and go over the station's Hoosier Hysteria coverage for Saturday's Semi State. There are some parts of the coverage plan with which I totally disagree. They want to fly Mike back in early Saturday morning and then have him go all day covering a Semi State. "You do realize that tonight we're going on until 1:15 AM with our special NCAA coverage? Stack won't get to bed until 3. He'll be operating on fumes!" It is indicated to me that during busy times like this we have to work hard.

That sets me off. I start blistering the cover off the phone. The satellite truck practically shakes as I get mad and rant and rave. Afterwards, I kick myself for carrying on like that. In the book, *God's Promises*, that I carry around, I look at James 1:19-20. "Always be willing to listen and slow to speak. Do not become angry easily, because anger will not help you live the right kind of life God wants." There's a WHOLE lot in the Bible that makes it clear that fools lose their cool. No doubt I've been a fool too many times, but since going on my Emmaus Walk, it has cut down considerably. Ephesians 4:26 talks about being sure to stop being angry before the end of the day. Sometimes it takes me until 11:59:59 PM but I've gotten better in that area too.

Within minutes, I call back and apologize to the decision maker for getting angry. As the rain pelts the satellite truck windows, I read Proverbs 14:29. "Patient people have great understanding, but people with quick tempers show their foolishness."

At 6:00 Mike Stack and I stand together outside in the driving rain and sleet for "team coverage." We only have one umbrella so I hold it as we get ready to go on air. By this time it's so cold and miserable that I have left my jacket in the truck and confiscated Wilson's burly work jacket. I look like Ivan from Russia, but I sure am warmer. We zip through our report and make a bee line back to the truck.

After the 6:00 Sports live, we catch our breath. We're not going live at 11:00 because CBS's NCAA coverage will not end until after midnight. The station wants us to send back a report that they will lead the late, late newscast with. I crank out a 2:20 package containing all of the elements we've accumulated.

Dead tired, we finally get to our hotel at 9:30 PM. It has been a 16-hour day. I tell Rick and Mike that we'll meet at 9:30 tomorrow morning. The station wants us to go live at noon, so we need to get back downtown and find something for that show.

Before heading back, I say good night to Wilson. He's a great guy. He handled satellite communications for telephones for part of his 22 years in the military. That background made him a good fit to become a satellite truck operator and engineer at WSBT. I'm always playing jokes on the jovial Wilson. In 1997 we took the truck to Bears training camp in Wisconsin. Wilson was bone weary from an 18-hour day. As he headed towards his hotel room I heard him say, "I sure hope the station doesn't call with breaking news that I have to be somewhere tomorrow morning..." I waited until I was sure Wilson was in his room and just in getting the pillows right. I rang his room.

"Hello," Wilson said slowly. The fatigue dripped from his voice.

"Wilson, this is Jim Freeman (WSBT president/general manager) at WSBT." Actually, it was me doing my Jim Freeman voice. I could just picture Wilson sitting up straight in bed, even though "Mr. Freeman" couldn't see him.

"Hello, sir! How are you?"

"Fine, Wilson. Listen, CBS needs the satellite truck back at the station by 6 AM tomorrow morning. That won't be a problem for you, will it?" I had to cover my mouth to keep Wilson from hearing me laugh. I could just picture him slumped over. To get the truck back at that early hour he would have to get right back out of bed and start driving to South Bend.

There was a long pause on Wilson's end.

"Uh, sir, I'll have it there. No...problem."

"Hey, Wilson. This is actually Charlie!"

"YOU RAT! I'LL GET YOU, CHARLIE!"

FRIDAY MARCH 20

Mike joins me for breakfast around 8:30 in the hotel restaurant. While making a point by waving my fork around, a chunk of scrambled egg comes off and flies into the wall. Thap! Everyone stares at me. They probably think I'm some wound-up business executive firing up my sales guy to reach quota that day.

At 9:30 AM, we're driving back to downtown St. Louis for another action-packed day. The station wants us to go live on the noon news-cast. An 11:50 AM satellite window has been ordered for us to send back some tape. When we pull into the Kiel Center parking lot at 10:00 AM, Wilson is already there and has the truck perculating.

Mike and I head over to the Hyatt at Union Station. That's where the Purdue team and fans are staying. We interview some Boilermaker fans about tonight's game with Stanford and then come back to the truck. Mike cranks out a piece for noon. Being the sharp guy that he is, Rick Stuckey went and bought us matching umbrellas. Now we look big time except that I'm still wearing Wilson's burly jacket and Mike is wear-ing his new spiffy overcoat. We notice that WISH hired a St. Louis tent company to come out and put together a big canvas party tent for their sportscasters to do their live shots in comfort.

In the afternoon, Mike and I drive over to The Regal which is the Valparaiso team hotel. It is a swirl of excitement. Valpo boosters are

grinning from ear to ear. Reaching the Sweet 16 has been an incredible experience. Every fan I interview praises the Valpo players for being gentlemen. One fella gives me a Valpo T-shirt. I promise to wear it on the air tonight. Lots of little kids are on the look-out for Bryce Drew. The 6' 4" senior has become quite a player through tremendous effort his whole life.

"He was not naturally gifted with great quickness or great speed," says Coach Homer Drew, "but he worked hard to compensate. He learned how to shoot and how to pass and how to understand the game of basketball. Bryce is a great success story for a lot of young people who dream whether it's baseball, basketball, soccer, or whatever sport, or whatever it might be—making A's in school or owning your own business. Whatever your dream is, it can come true with hard work and dedication toward that goal you have."

Ironically, before this magical season started, Homer granted behind-the-scenes access to writer Shawn Malayter to do a book. The title is "*Find A Way* ": *Valpo's Sweet Dream* to be published by South Bend's very own sports publisher (and mine!), Diamond Communications, Inc.

After getting plenty of good material, Mike and I drive to the Gateway Arch where I shoot a standup between the arches. Mike will put this story together to lead the 5:00 newscast. The big Purdue pep rally doesn't start until 5:00 at a nearby tavern. I want that to be one of the elements of the 6:00 News coverage, so Mike hustles over and shoots the first 15 minutes of the rally. He makes it back to edit that to send back at 5:50. At 5:59, I'm standing at our live shot location listening to WSBT through my I.F.B. earpiece. At 6:00, just one minute before they are to come to me, my I.F.B. goes out. Something happened. There's no way I can go live unless I can hear them. In the satellite truck, Wilson furiously redials the I.F.B. number. There's nothing I can do but stand there and hope I'm reconnected. If not, they can "float" me in the show. That means the news anchors can read a couple of news stories that were intended to be after me. Then, when I'm reconnected, they can come to me live. Wilson comes through, though, and I'm reconnected 10 seconds before I come on live. I hear anchors Cindy Ward and Mike Collins through my earpiece and everything ends up going fine. The viewer at home has no idea that we walked a tightrope there.

My 6:00 newscast appearance includes two v/o's (voice overs).

On air, I say, "Let's check out the Purdue rally, which is still going on." In a satellite live shot, I cannot see the video on a monitor, so the producer tells me through my ear piece that "the video is up." I then ad lib about the spirit of the rally and how Purdue is trying to make it to the Final Four for the first time since 1980.

After the 6:00 live shots end, we all head into the Kiel Center to plow through some of the buffet. The media is served dinner at the very top of the arena. We have a breathtaking view off the basketball court. I almost feel like I should be strapped in because when you look over the table railing, it's a complete drop off.

Just before tipoff of Purdue-Stanford, I find my media seat. It's right next to the Purdue bench. Seated next to me is a St. Louis radio man. When he realizes that I am from Indiana he has many questions about Indiana high school basketball. This happens to me at every NCAA Tourney I cover. The media from that state are often in awe of Hoosier Hysteria and drill me with questions on it.

Early on I notice something that goes basically unnoticed in the media coverage of the game. The rims at the Kiel Center are the tightest I've seen in a long time. After one minute of play I know Chad Austin is going to have a bad game. His jump shot is low trajectory. These rims will not be kind to line drive jump shots. Sure enough, Purdue makes only six of 29 three-point attempts. Austin makes only four of 18 baskets. Stanford kills them on the boards and gets a lot of their points on rebound baskets. Stanford makes only four of 16 three-point attempts, but ends up beating Purdue, 67-59.

Afterwards, I meet Rick outside the Purdue locker room to do interviews. As a mob of media stands patiently, NCAA officials bark out, "Stand back! Stand back! Up against the wall!"

You'd think President Clinton or Leonardo DiCaprio was coming through. Instead, it's the referees. The NCAA takes itself WAY too seriously during the tournament. The locker room finally opens and we start doing interviews. Purdue center Brad Miller is slumped over. "We can't interview him now," I tell Rick. "He's inaudible. The guy is so torn up he's barely whispering when answering the questions." Miller was beaten silly by those thugs that call themselves basketball players at Stanford.

Jaraan Cornell handles himself gallantly during my interview with him. He addresses everything head on and makes no excuses. We also interview Purdue's Mike Robinson ("We got our butts kicked"), Alan Eldridge (he didn't buy into my tight rim theory), and eventually Miller. As we leave, I'm struck by the sight of the Purdue assistant coaches in a separate room. They are devastated. Each one slumps over a chair exhausted. They spent so much time preparing for this game. With Kansas having been knocked out of the Midwest Regionals, they knew they had a very good chance of reaching the Final Four. The disappointment of coming up short will not leave them for a long time.

Rick and Mike head to the truck to edit together the sound bites to send back to South Bend for our late newscast. I head back into the arena and am standing there as Valpo runs back onto the court for starting introductions. Bryce Drew and the Crusaders run right past me. I get goosebumps as the crowd roars. My "tight rim" theory comes through again. Rhode Island players appear to have much more arch on their shots than Valpo players. They drop in some three-point bombs. That, and their fierce defense, is too much for the Crusaders as their Cinderella run expires. With eight minutes to go, I leave and head across to the satellite truck. I watch the final moments there as we get set to go on live when CBS ends its NCAA coverage. I call WSBT and talk with producer Jim Pinkerton.

"You have the coordinates for Homer's postgame press conference, don't you?" I ask Jim.

"We're all set," he responds. "We'll tape it here."

The plan is for me to introduce my Purdue interviews live then send it back to Mike and Cindy. They will introduce the Homer Drew interview from there.

"Why don't I intro the Homer stuff from here?" I ask Jim. "I am in St. Louis."

"We've already got it written for the anchors," he says.

"Having already imploded and had a temper fit yesterday, I back off. It's not worth hassling over. CBS finally ends its coverage at 12:45 AM. We are live off and on in the newscast until 1:15 AM. During Sports, I light into the Big Ten Conference.

"Once again, it underachieves in the Big Dance," I bark out. "They came up with that silly Big Ten Tourney to toughen up their teams. What a joke. End that goofy Big Ten Tourney. It's a greed thing anyway. If the Big Ten is to get the respect of the ACC, SEC, and Pac Ten, it has got to get its act together and do better in the NCAA's!" Half of my little commentary is accurate. Half of it is because I'm bone tired and standing in the rain again.

The show ends at 1:18 and we plop down in the truck. Wilson lowers the satellite dish from on top of the truck and listens as I get Matt on the phone.

"Here's the deal for tomorrow," I say. "Plymouth is playing the morning game in the Muncie Semi State. Wilson will stay here in St. Louis at his hotel until the Plymouth game ends. Matt, when it is over, you call Wilson. If Plymouth wins, Wilson and the truck go to Muncie. That way we'll be able to feed back coverage of their Semi State championship game. If Plymouth loses in the morning game, he'll head back to South Bend."

Mike, Rick, and I get back to our hotel around 3:00 AM. It's been an 18 $\frac{1}{2}$ hour day. Had Purdue and/or Valpo won, we would have covered their press conferences on Saturday and then covered the Elite Eight game on Sunday. With them eliminated, we now will call the airlines and try to get an early flight back to South Bend. That's how it is covering the NCAA's. If your team or teams are bounced, it's time to head home.

MARCH
Tuesday
24

Pat Garrity on Work Ethic and Reflections from a South Bend Sportswriting Hall-of-Famer

CBS Sports in New York calls and asks us to interview Notre Dame basketball star Pat Garrity. They're running a Final Four special before Saturday's coverage. They want us to ask Garrity about being the GTE Academic All-American of the Year. Garrity has a 3.68 grade point average in Pre-Professional Science. They also want Garrity to talk about developing into one of the top college players in America. Coming out of high school in Monument, Colorado, Garrity was not rated among the super dooper recruits. "There's no magic formula," Garrity tells our Mike Stack as the camera rolls. "It was just hours alone in repetitions in the gym where I was able to improve myself to a level I didn't even think I would be able to get to. The same thing follows for what's going to happen in the next few years [NBA]. I'm going to have to keep doing that kind of thing if I'm going to get better." When asked what advice he would give to young people about having academic success in school, Garrity said, "Get on top of it early—the first couple of weeks. It's just like sports. You can get confidence early." Garrity then reflected on four years of academic and basketball excellence at Notre Dame. "As I look back, it shows me I really took full advantage of the programs the university offers. I didn't short change myself and be one dimensional. I took full advantage of being a college student-athlete. It says for Notre Dame

Chopper Charlie and pilot Brian Riley of Riley Aviation in Sturgis, Michigan.

Charlie rattles away at the famous Big Board.

Sports reporter Mike Stack (left) and weekend sports anchor Matt Burridge in the WSBT Sports office.

Command Central—The WSBT Sports office.

Rick Mecklenburg, the pride of Niles, works with some of his stormtracker equipment in the Weather office.

News Director Meg Sauer and Executive Producer Tim Ceravolo plan WSBT's new 5:30 newscast.

Charlie and news anchor Amanda Hart tape a promo for the new 5:30 newscast they'll anchor together.

WSBT Nightshift editor Tony Fuller helps put together "Friday Night Fever."

Charlie and meteorologist Rick Mecklenburg apply makeup for the evening news.

Engineer Wilson Johnson and Mike Stack work in the WSBT satellite truck during the NCAA Basketball Tournament.

Charlie sports a goofy grin next to Indiana native David Letterman.

Mike Stack talks to the crowd enjoying the flag football game during En-shrinement Weekend at the College Football Hall of Fame.

Charlie poses with Coach Mike Ditka.

At the College Football Hall of Fame, Charlie interviews Liz Heaston, the first woman to ever play in a men's college football game.

Chopper Charlie becomes Peyton Manning as he throws footballs to the fans in Dowagiac, Michigan.

The Adamses—Jack, Sherrad, Charlie, and Abigail. (Photos by Joyce)

that Coach MacLeod and everyone in the program is focused on academics. It says we recruit the kind of people that are all about academics. Serious about basketball, but also serious about getting a degree."

One of our other stories today is on retired *South Bend Tribune* sportswriter Bob Towner. On Friday he's going to be inducted into the Indiana Sportswriters and Sportscasters Hall of Fame in Greenwood, Indiana. Bob covered Sports for the *Tribune* from 1941 to 1983. In the late afternoon, Mike goes to Bob's house in Clay Township to interview him about his 47 years of sportswriting for two newspapers.

"Ever since I was a junior high kid I knew what I wanted to do and was very fortunate to be able to do it," Bob says. As for his advice to those in any profession: "Don't lose your enthusiasm. When you've lost that, you've lost just about everything."

We asked Bob to name the best athletes he knew of during his sportswriting days. "The best high school football player is one I never saw play prep ball—Ernie Zalejski of Washington. From all accounts he was undoubtedly among the very best. His records say so. I was 'busy' with World War II when Ernie was scoring touchdowns, but I did see him play for Notre Dame after the war. He was then hampered with injury.

"Perhaps the best all-around athlete was Riley High's Ole Galloway. He was the first named the Most Valuable Player in our Northern Indiana Conference TWICE—in 1964 and 1965. Ole also won four (if memory serves) state prep wrestling championships. He was a baseball star, too, hitting well over .400."

We asked Bob about the best teams he covered. "Wow, there were lots. Old Central High School's history is dotted with 'em. My favorite is the 1973 Washington High team coached by Bob (Beans) Van Camp because it won the very first on-the-field playoff championship in the Class AAA category. Washington beat Indianapolis Cathedral 19-13. Mike Miller had a seven-yard touchdown run, a 22-yard interception return for a touchdown, and a key interception with 2:27 to go. The Panthers controlled the ball, but the game's final play was bizarre and almost gave the game away. With the clock ticking away the final seconds, quarterback Al Rzepka took a deliberate delay of game penalty, pushing the ball back to the Indianapolis 44. Rzepka was now faced with fourth down, 11 yards to go, and only six seconds showing on the clock. He took the snap from center Dean Downer and began to race toward his own goal. He reached his own 20 when the clock showed 0:00. The packed crowd at School Field and the pressbox personnel gasped as, with a mighy heave, he threw the ball toward the Washington sideline, not realizing the ball could have been intercepted and returned for a possible enemy touchdown. As it was, an Indianapolis defender did get his hands on the ball.

An understanding Coach Van Camp put the final spin on the play when he said: 'All Al wanted to do was to get the game ball to me on the sideline.'"

Bob reflected to us about covering the week-long Western Junior tennis tourney at Notre Dame and how Coach Tom Fallon sat beside him for a week, teaching him about the game. "The Notre Dame football teams of the post-War II Era fashioned that great 39-game streak without defeat that Purdue finally ended," Bob recalled. "I still remember *Tribune* editor Ed Young's famous headline on that occasion: 'Irish Upset.' And he placed it upside down at the top of the page."

We asked Bob for some dirt on longtime *Tribune* sports editor Joe Doyle. "Joe and I worked together for 30 years and I don't remember a cross word ever between us. We got along beautifully. He is highly sought after as an expert and historian of Notre Dame football and deservedly so. His file of memories is fantastic."

"How about a bizarre story you covered, Bob?"

"My sports editor (long ago and not Joe) asked me to do a piece on Clashmore Mike, then the Irish terrier mascot of Notre Dame football teams. Joe Dierickx was the old stadium caretaker and Clashmore Mike keeper. I interviewed that dog, fed him some chocolate, and interpreted his barks into a column. It was fun and he was a polite canine...didn't bite."

We asked Bob about his relationship with Notre Dame football coaches and administrators. "As a group, Notre Dame football coaches were great. They always had time for us. Ara used to have conferences just for the area writers. As everyone will tell you, Gerry Faust was probably the most friendly. Among the assistants my favorites were George Kelly (first knew him at St. Joseph's High), Joe Yonto, and Tom Pagna— and not in particular order. Moose Krause was without parallel as a coach, athletic director, and friend. Always a generous smile and the famous cigar."

Lloyd Carr on Success

Mike Stack points the WSBT camera at the white curtain in the Great Hall of Century Center. Behind the curtain is something large and oval shaped. Please, don't let it be Godzilla's child. At 10:45 AM we anxiously watch as the curtain unveils and out comes Sideline Sam! It's the brand new mascot of the College Football Hall of Fame. It looks like a distant cousin of the Planter's Peanut thing. Sideline Sam is seven feet tall and shaped like a football. He dances around the podium as the third graders of Mrs. Jean Watts' class at Christ the King cheer loudly. They were the ones that came up with the mascot's name.

After all the commotion dies down, I walk over with Mike and interview Mrs. Watts about how her class came up with the winning nickname. "We took about two days," she says, as third graders stand all around waving at the WSBT camera. "We took it real seriously. We had a whole board of football words. We brainstormed and talked about it. We got into groups and came up with four good names. We had a voting process and came up with Sideline Sam." Among their other "finalist" names were Fullback Fred and Cubee Jack. "I was into that name," Mrs. Watts says of Cubee (rhymes with QB) Jack. Meredith Monserez was the student that came up with Sideline Sam. "I saw the name 'sideline' on the board and we just thought 'Sam' because both start with an 's.'" Sounds good to me!

Meanwhile, 470 college football fans have arrived to hear Michigan coach Lloyd Carr be the guest speaker for this month's Gridiron Legends luncheon. The ticket demand was so strong that it had to be moved from the College Football Hall of Fame to the Great Hall at Century Center. At the podium, Carr looks out at the students from area High Schools and Middle Schools. "Young people," he says with a smile, "choose something for a career that you LOVE to do. If not, you'll find disappointment."

Listening to Carr, it's obvious why Michigan won the National Championship. The Wolverines were a true team. "The team had one heartbeat," Carr said, referring to how Bear Bryant once described his Alabama team. Carr tells the audience about Eric Mayes. He came to Michigan as a walk-on linebacker at 5' 9," 215 pounds. "He was always told he wasn't big enough or fast enough," Carr says. "As a junior, he got on the kickoff coverage team because of injuries. He ended up securing a spot on Special Teams. Then in the spring we had a kid drop out who had been one of the most highly recruited players when he came to Michigan. I looked over in practice and there was Eric in the starting linebacker spot. That August, he was selected captain. I believe he is the first walk-on in the history of Michigan football to be voted captain. Then in the fourth game of his senior year (against Indiana), Eric tore his knee up. His season was over as far as playing. But just five days after his operation, he was back at every meeting and practice and continued to lead this team!"

Carr gives a well-paced motivational talk in a style that's befitting of his low-key manner. He doesn't raise his voice or wave his arms. He simply gets it across plainly that if your organization wants success, then you have to be a true team like the 1997 Wolverines. Carr quotes Harry Truman, Franklin Roosevelt, Scott Peck, and others. He recites poems with motivational elements. At no point does he ever read from his notes. "In society, too often winning is the only thing," Carr says sincerely. "In 1948 Harry Truman was asked about success. He said out in Tombstone, Arizona, there's an epitaph that reads, 'Here lies Jack Williams. He done his damndest.'" Carr pauses. "That's success! Fame is a vapor. The only thing that endures is character."

As I sit there at the media table, it makes me think of another thing basketball star Pat Garrity said in reflecting on his days at Notre Dame.

He said in time people would not remember as much about his basketball statistics and awards, but they would always remember how he carried himself on and off the court. Carr is right. Character endures.

After the luncheon ends, Mike and I drive out to Notre Dame for Bob Davie's Spring Football news conference. Davie says the most disappointing thing of the 7-6 record in the 1997 season was their tentativeness. Aggressiveness in every area will be the foundation of the 1998 Irish. Back at WSBT, I have Sideline Sam come to the station about 4:45 for a live appearance during the 5:00 newscast. Before airtime, I guide Sam around the station. This is a surprise to the folks in Sales upstairs. While they're on the phone closing a deal, I have Sideline Sam walk into their office and hug them.

At the end of the 5:00 News, I prod Sideline Sam to mess up Luke Choate's bionic hair. If I did this to a news anchor in a top market, he would keel over from shock and call his therapist and agent. Not Luke, he rolls with the punches because he's such a genuinely nice guy. I would never do this during a serious part of the newscast, but it's fine at the very end.

After the 6:00 newscast, I meet the family at Evangel Heights for Wednesday night spaghetti. It's a great opportunity for midweek fellowship with folks at church. Sherrad and the kids and I end up kicking the soccer ball around in the Rec Room there until about 8:00. I then say goodbye and head back to the station to get the 11:00 newscast together. It's tough leaving the family like this. That's why I'm looking forward to going dayside so much.

A Pioneer in Her Sport

It's a good thing I'm at work a little early today. At 1:45, I check my voice mail. The College Football Hall of Fame has called to say a very interesting guest is there for an hour or so. It's the first woman to ever play in a men's college football game. With tailback speed, I zip into the newsroom and spot my buddy, news reporter Ray Roth. "Hey, Ray! Are you doing anything?"

"Not really," he responds. "Just getting set to edit my 6:00 News story."

"Grab your gear and let's go the Hall!"

Ray has never been to the Hall of Fame, so he quickly gets into the plan. Within five minutes, we're on the bottom level of the Hall looking for Liz Heaston, who made sports history on October 18, 1997. She kicked two extra points for Willamette (Oregon) University in a win over Linfield College. The usual kicker for Willamette was injured, so their head coach Dan Hawkins recruited Liz from the soccer team to kick for the football team that week. A Hall of Fame official finds us and tells us Liz is in the Stadium Theatre. That's an incredible part of the Hall experience, so we wait patiently while the pulse pounding action on the screens goes on inside.

Within minutes, the 5' 5" college junior emerges. She's not in shoulder pads, but in a long dress with high heels. Highly articulate, she explains that she has been in Chicago earlier in the day looking at eye doctor schools. Knowing her cleats and jersey were on display at the Hall, she and her mother wanted to take the opportunity of coming over from Chicago to South Bend to see them and the rest of the Hall.

Ken Fox of the *South Bend Tribune* is there also. I suggest we go to the field goal area of the Hall to do the interview. With goalposts behind her, Liz explains about her success kicking in a men's college football game. "Women kickers can do the job," she says confidently. "As soccer players, we have to be more accurate because playing soccer you have to hit people rather than a big wide open area (the space between the goal posts). Kicking extra points is a very accomplishable goal for females." Liz tells us of another woman who kicked an extra point for a men's team in a NAIA game a few weeks after her kick. She's also heard of a division-one men's program in Florida that is looking for a woman kicker to kick extra points. I ask Liz if she can come over to WSBT for a live in-studio appearance on Weekday SportsBeat. That sounds great to her and her mother. They're not leaving South Bend until early evening.

Back at WSBT I tell SportsBeat co-host Tom Dennin about Liz being in town and that I asked her to be on his show. It's Tom and John Fineran's show, but from time to time if I run into interesting potential guests I go ahead and line them up. Tom thinks it's a great idea and pores over Liz' background information from a press release I've brought him.

During a break in SportsBeat, I ask Liz what advice she would give young female athletes. "Believe in yourself," she says. "Be determined. Know there's going to be a lot of hard work, but if you have ability, go for it! You can reach for the stars and grab them. They're there!" She tells me since her kicks, at least eight women applicants to Willamette University have put "football" on their applications.

After the radio show, I call the CBS sports video feed in New York and ask them if they have any file video of Liz. Sure enough, they put her historic kicks on the 10:15 PM night video feed. That really jazzes up the story I do on her for the late newscast. Afterwards, anchor Mike Collins says he noticed that both snaps were bad and Liz had to adjust her kicking style. She still boomed them through the uprights. The video shows the stands were packed for the game. Camera crews were all over the place.

Ironically, six months after Liz visits South Bend, Riley High School's Allison Nickle makes history by becoming the first female varsity kicker in South Bend.

APRIL
Wednesday
1

Taking on the Elkhart Fire Department

The WSBT TV/Sunny 101.5 FM All-Star Basketball team is headed to Elkhart for a charity basketball game. We're "playing" against the Elkhart Fire Department with the money raised going to the Survive Alive House. This program will be taken all over the county to educate kids and the elderly about what to do in case of a fire. It's going to have strobe lights in it that simulate a fire. It will have heated doors, and they'll be able to pump in video smoke. Anyone going through it will know just what to do if a fire ever breaks out in their home. There's already a Survive Alive House in Clay Township that's been drawing rave reviews.

I'm going to do the 5:00 and 6:00 sportscasts live from the gym at Pierre Moran Middle School on West Lusher Street in Elkhart. On nights like this I don't really have a chance to eat, so on the way over I cruise into the drive through at Penguin Point Restaurant to get some of their people-pleasing chicken.

At the gym I plow through the chicken, which I was told at the drive-through window is "fresh and never frozen." I then spend some time talking with Elkhart fire chief Tony Johnson, who has been a driving force behind the Survive Alive House. He shows me a check for $1,000 from Black Expo that's been donated. Also on hand is Elkhart

Fire Department deputy chief Tony Cinelli. Standing next to Tony Johnson, Cinelli tells me about their remarkable similarities. "We both have wives named Susan," Cinelli says. "We both have children named Michael. We both went to Pierre Moran here. We're just three months apart in age."

Cinelli tells me the most important thing for fire prevention for kids is NOT TO PLAY WITH MATCHES or anything like a match. He also shares something I'd never realized. If a fire has broken out in a family home, kids need to know that amidst all the smoke the firefighters will look like "something out of a strange country" in all their gear. They don't mean to look imposing, but they might come across that way. "It's important that when kids see us in a fire to not hide from us," Cinelli says.

Around 6:45 the citizens of Elkhart start pouring through the door to support the game and the cause. Raffle tickets are sold. Bob Davie and John MacLeod have generously donated autographed balls. There's no telling how much money is raised for various charities because of autographs from the famous coaches at Notre Dame through the years.

Playing for us will be Bethel College star Rico Swanson. An ultra special player, Rico just wrapped up a historic career for the Pilots that saw him lead them to three National Championships. Our roster cracks me up. We've got an incredible player in Rico to go along with a bunch of creaky "talent challenged" TV and radio folks.

The Elkhart Fire Department has a bunch of strong, strappin' ball players. Glancing at them in warmups, I turn to Rico. "Shoot the ball every time you get it, Rico," I plead. "And don't ever, EVER pass it to Ed Ernstes."

Rico goes on to put on a show. He fires in 41 points from all over the court. His shots are spectacular and Jordan-esque. Still, we trail at the half. During the intermission, I sell 12 WSBT autographed coffee cups for $5 each. "Cindy Ward has actually touched these cups," I chirp as I peddle the cups. The money goes to the cause. Audrey Stouder of Elkhart says she'll buy one if I give her a kiss. Drenched with sweat, I go up into the stands and plant one on her cheeks. I then apologize that Ed Ernstes wore shorts revealing his pasty white legs.

To make the second half more competitive, the fire department puts on their bulky firefighting jackets for half of the third quarter. They proceed to lose about eight gallons of sweat while Rico launches a series of three-point baskets. The game is tied with two minutes to go, but Ed Ernstes checks back in for WSBT and we go on to lose.

Afterwards, young kids from Elkhart swarm Rico to get autographs. Rico will go down as one of the great athletes to ever come out of South Bend. He's also a class act to drive over on his own and play in the benefit game.

If you would like the Survive Alive House to come to your school or function in Elkhart County, then give them a call at the Elkhart Fire Department.

APRIL
Sunday
5

Coverage at Augusta National, Site of the Masters

Due to the kindness and generosity of WSBT management, it has been my privilege to go to Augusta National the past five years. I never will forget my first trip to the sight of The Masters in 1994. As soon as I arrived on the grounds, I briskly walked to Amen Corner. It was late in the afternoon on a Tuesday and most of the gallery had left for the day. Only a few golfers were still on the course practicing. I was virtually by myself as I stood alongside the 11th fairway and looked down at the Par 3 12th hole, the hole where Fred Couples' ball barely stayed out of the water the year he won a Green Jacket. Rae's Creek and the two famous bridges seemed almost larger than life. I then angled over to the Par 5, 13th hole, which has always been my favorite one. A tributary of Rae's Creek crawls in front of the green on 13. The azaleas and dogwoods were peaking during tournament week that year. When you combine the beauty of the towering pines, dogwoods and azaleas with the unlimited budget that goes into maintaining Amen Corner and the rest of the course, it will make you take two steps backwards with semi-awe. I'm not kidding when I say I was so excited that my breathing resembled Luke Choate trying to finish a 10K. My heart beat raced a mile a minute. Generally, not many things in sports have floored me since adulthood, but coming to Augusta National in person certainly affected me. That was 1994. This year, sports reporter Mike Stack is flying down with me. As we board the airplane, an elderly lady in the back instantly recognizes me. As I help Mike put the camera in the overhead compartment, she starts up about my "on air" work. She is very complimentary, but that's the "problem." In a voice that can be heard all over the plane, she keeps referring to me as "big boy" as she carries on about watching WSBT News. Everyone on the plane looks up from their newspaper and stares at me. I consider getting in the overhead compartment with the camera.

We land in Atlanta at noon and immediately rent a car. Within 20 minutes we're parking next to Turner Field, home of the Atlanta Braves. Passing Hall-of-Fame pitcher Don Sutton on our way into the Braves' press box, Mike and I settle down for what will be a masterpiece. Greg Maddux is pitching for Atlanta. Curt Schilling goes for the Phillies. Schilling strikes out 15 Braves. Maddux has pinpoint control, as usual. They are so dominant the game goes only two hours and seven minutes. The Phillies win a pitching classic, 2-1.

In the April 6th edition of the *Atlanta Journal-Constitution*, Steve Hummer would write, "You say something's got to be done to speed up baseball? When Maddux and Schilling were finished with their 127-minute workday Sunday, the game felt entirely too short, like a concert without encores. You say today's players just don't care about the product, that they're only in it for the thousands of dollars they draw with every breath. Put them behind a couple pitchers who are highly-infectious carriers of excellence, and see how interested they become."

I'd much rather see a drama-filled, build-up-the-tension game like this than some of these 14-11 slugfests.

Afterwards, Mike and I make the two-and-a-half hour drive on 1-20 East to Augusta. Mike has never been to Augusta National so as we pull into the city I drive by the exterior. He gets a brief glance down Magnolia Lane. As our car moves past the entrance, Mike sees the clubhouse for a split second at the end of the famous driveway. He can't wait until tomorrow morning when we go inside. We then drive to the house we'll be staying in for the three days of practice rounds. A lot of families in Augusta rent out their homes to media and the players. They charge an arm and a leg and take off for a week. The Augusta Schools even plan spring break for Masters week. The house we're in is about four miles from the course. It's a charming, well-decorated middle income home in a neighborhood filled with pines. I "assign" Mike to the teenage boys room (single bed) and I take the master bedroom. Hey, I'm 6' 5," 230. I can't fit on a youngster's bed. My feet would hang over. Veteran sportswriters Phil Richards of the *Indianapolis Star* and Stan Sutton of the *Louisville Courier* also share the house with us. They'll be getting in tomorrow. One of my Masters traditions at the rental house is immediately turning on Augusta cable to channel 4. That's the Real Estate channel. A man named Bob Hale is always on there pitching homes. He's a character seemingly out of "Sanford and Son." Bob carries on about how prospective home buyers in Augusta need to get away from "the Rent Man" and buy a house from him. He's seen driving an old ambulance by the road where a man is lying down covered with a sheet. Bob Hale gets out and surveys the man. "This man is a victim of STICKER SHOCK!" he exclaims. Bob goes on to explain the man has keeled over because the houses he was looking at were way too expensive. Bob then gives the man a shot and up he pops. Bob then takes him to some of *his* houses for sale. To me, Bob Hale is as much a part of Masters week as the Par 3 contest, Amen Corner, and the awarding of the Green Jacket.

Mike and I sit in the den and watch the numerous half hour specials on The Masters. Every local TV station does extensive coverage all week. The Augusta paper devotes four sections in its Sunday paper to previewing The Masters. The event deserves it. The Masters is the hottest ticket in all of sports.

MONDAY APRIL 6

By 6:30 AM, we're headed out the door of our rental house to famed Augusta National. We're on a tight schedule. By 11:30 AM we've got to have a lot of material shot and ready to edit. We'll be working out of the satellite truck of WGNX-TV of Atlanta. WSBT assignment editor John Snyder did a great job in lining up their truck for us to edit in and uplink our stories back to South Bend. Because the truck is also being used by the CBS Sports Feed, we've been told we need to do our editing from 11:30 to 1:30. That gives us a sense of urgency.

As we pull into the massive parking lot at 6:50 AM, a line of fans stretches 300 yards. They can't get in yet, but they're already in line.

Many of these folks are seeing Augusta National for the first time and you can see the excitement in their eyes. They wrote for applications for a practice round ticket a few years ago and now their name has been drawn. Virtually everyone has a camera in hand and a fat wallet to buy souvenirs at the gift shop.

Waves of Pinkerton Security guards stand at the entrance. There's no way someone could slide in without a gallery badge or media credential. The guards' eyes constantly scan everyone that enters. Mike and I flash our paper credential, which gets us to the Media Center. There, they give us each a Media I.D. that we pin to our shirts.

Mike's eyes are darting everywhere. The experience is overwhelming to a first-time visitor. With a WSBT News 22 camera in hand, we walk alongside the 10th fairway. It drops down much more than is evident when you watch on CBS. Groundskeepers are attending to every inch of the course. To me, Augusta National is as close to perfect as any large piece of land I've ever seen. There are many places like Pebble Beach that offer more natural beauty but no place comes even close to being as well kept as this place. At the 12th hole, Mike and I crank out several "stand ups" to be inserted into our coverage that day. We then walk back to the practice range area in pursuit of interviews. Within minutes, 1996 Western Amateur champion Joel Kribel comes by and enthusiastically responds to our request for an interview. Joel tells me he has chills going down his spine. "It's a feeling like none other," he says of being in his first Masters. "I've been in awe." Joel's a very polite young man who qualified for this year's Masters by being runnerup in the 1997 U.S. Amateur. I ask him how Augusta National compares to Point O' Woods in Benton Harbor, site of the prestigious Western Amateur.

"The courses are actually pretty similar," Joel says. "Tiger Woods said the Western Amateur is the Masters of Amateur Golf. That speaks volumes for the Western Am. The course at Point O' Woods is an awesome golf course. It has really fast greens like they are here."

I thank Joel for his time and he heads towards the putting green. His comments back up my feelings that more people in the South Bend area should go to the Western Am every year in late July.

Within moments, three-time Masters champion Gary Player comes bouncing by us. The South African is always upbeat and willing to talk.

During the interview, another TV reporter asks him if an older golfer will ever win The Masters.

"One day a man of 60 will win Augusta," Player says confidently. "Of course, in today's modern era, one cannot adjust his mind to say that will happen. If you speak to gerontologists, people will be living to 130 years of age with diet and exercise and mindset. That's going to happen. So a man of 60 one day will be the equivilant of a man of 30 today. That's medical fact."

Gary means business when it comes to clean living. I even see his caddy munching on an apple.

Gary not only talks the talk, he walks the walk. The 62-year-old goes on later in the week to become the oldest man to *ever* make the cut at The Masters.

With interviews in tow, Mike and I walk back out to the parking lot area where all the satellite trucks are parked. I plop down inside the spacious WGNX Truck and carve out several stories based on all the tape we've shot that morning. While I edit, Mike takes the gear back to the course and shoots two features that will run later in the week. By late afternoon, we get in our rental car and go get a bite to eat on Washington Road. I eat fast because I want to get to our rental house so I can turn on Bob Hale on the Real Estate Channel.

TUESDAY APRIL 7

Mike Stack and I are back at Augusta National by 6:45 AM. Our plan is to get some interviews with the golfers before they start playing practice rounds at 8 AM. We have immediate success as Big John Daly ambles from the practice range right towards us. His buddy Fuzzy Zoeller is right behind him. Stack hoists the camera to his shoulder as I ask Daly for an interview. He smiles and shakes my hand. Despite his well-publicized problems in the past with alcohol and "rearranging the furniture in rooms," Daly is a nice guy who means well. Realizing he's headed towards the first tee, I stay away from questions on his battle against alcohol. Besides, there have been many lengthy print and broadcast stories on that subject. I ask him about how well he's playing (at the time he's leading the PGA Tour in putting and driving) and if he has lost any steam off the tee with his "grip it and rip it" driving style. "It's been a little longer," Daly says, "but a little straighter too. That's kind of nice and that's because of the driver I'm using, the Callaway. It just makes it a lot easier to play." Afterwards, I shake hands and thank him for his time. Daly smiles again and catches up to Fuzzy. It's been a year since Daly has taken a drink. His ballmarkers are special coins given to him by fellow Alcoholics Anonymous members which reflect the length of their sobriety.

Now that I've interviewed Daly, I need some video of him to make the story work. Stack and I walk to the first tee and wait for them to tee off. Daly launches a rocket 300 yards over the massive fairway bunker that sits about 250 yards from the tee. While walking to get in position for his second shot, we run into Mike Basney and Mike Grabovez from South Bend. They've come along with some friends for some golf in Georgia as well as a trip inside Augusta National. I ask Basney what he thinks of this place. "It's the mecca of golf," Basney says. "Every golfer in the world wants to be here and see this event. This is probably the finest golf course you'll ever see."

We follow Daly through the first two holes, which gives us plenty of video to use. Then we make the walk back towards the clubhouse. As soon as we return, Greg Norman emerges from the players' locker room and strides directly towards us. He's going to the practice green. Knowing that Norman doesn't do many one-on-one interviews I'm inclined not to ask him for one, but Stack nudges me and says, "What the heck? The worst thing he can do is say 'no.'" I don't have any time to think about it. Norman is five feet from me.

"Greg, can I ask you a couple of questions?"

Norman comes to an abrupt halt and flashes me his icy stare. His steely eyes can bore laser holes through your skull when he wants to lock you in.

"What about?!" he answers back.

At this point my answer options are:

(1) "What the heck were you and President Clinton doing when he got hurt at your place?"

(2) "I would like you to painstakingly take me through how the wheels fell off when you lost your six-stroke lead to Nick Faldo in 1996."

(3) "I'd like to ask you about how your golf game is looking now."

I take option three and he surprisingly walks over to me. He's probably stunned some medium market crew with a 22 on their microphone flag had the gall to ask him for an interview. Stack opens with a two-shot of Norman and me. That way I can edit that in later and look like a big shot. Norman gives me a nice answer about coming back from a strained left shoulder which caused him to drop out of the recent Players Championship. I then ask him about Daly's recent return to golf. Daly missed last years Masters because he was in alcohol rehab. "He's recognized the problems he has got and I admire that in a man who can stand out there in front of the public and admit to his faults and turn around and try to change them," Norman says, with genuine care coming across. "Anytime one does that he gets a much better peace of mind and I think that's why his golf is getting better and better and it won't be long before you see John back in the winner's circle. We hope he gets back as fast as he can because he's a damn good guy."

I shake hands with Norman and thank him for his time. He nods and resumes his bee line walk towards the practice green. Hundreds of fans have stood behind the gallery ropes watching this interview. They snap dozens of pictures as Norman goes by them. As Mike and I put our WSBT microphone back in the bag, Michael Gleeson of Seven Network in Australia approaches us. "That's amazing," he says. "Norman usually never does interviews with just one crew like that."

Gleeson asks us for a dub of the interview which we give him later in the satellite truck. He uplinks it to Australia where the Channel 22 microphone flag is seen on their evening broadcast.

On a roll, Mike and I meander towards the players' locker room building. Several caddies wait outside to see what their respective golfer wants to do. Standing amongst them is "Fluff," the recognizable caddy of Tiger Woods. His overhanging walrus-like mustache makes him easy to spot. Fluff obliges to do an interview but right from the outset it's obvious he's not going to say much. Earlier in the week, I'd read in the Augusta paper that Ben Crenshaw had spent some time watching Tiger putt. There have been reports that Tiger's putting is not quite in sync. Fluff bristles when I ask him about Crenshaw. "You people in the media see two guys together and you think you know what's going on," Fluff gruffs. "Tiger's putting is fine."

Having plenty of material to work with, Mike and I walk back out to the course to do "stand ups" for our coverage. Jack Nicklaus and Arnold Palmer are playing a practice round, so we end up walking with their gallery for a few holes. Nicklaus and Palmer kid and zing each other as they go along, much to the gallery's delight. Mike marvels at watching the two greats play together. It's a special thing to see.

In the late afternoon, we stop at Applebee's on Washington Road (which is the Grape Road of Augusta) to get something to eat. I also use their phone to call in on Weekday SportsBeat on WSBT AM 960. I ask the nearby bartender to refrain from using his dacquiri machine while I'm on the phone. The contraption makes more noise than a jack-hammer. During the show, I have my interviews with Daly and Norman play to the radio audience. With tongue in cheek, I say that "I spent some time with Greg Norman" as I introduce that interview segment. Norman wouldn't remember me from Adam if he saw me, but I carry on like I'm Mr. Schmoozer with the big-timers.

While glancing at the Atlanta paper that evening at our rental house, the Braves-Pirates game is on TBS. I happen to hear announcer Pete Van Wieren say the Greg Maddux-Curt Schilling classic we saw in person "may have been the best pitching battle ever in Atlanta."

How about that. Ironically, in 1997, former WSBT sports reporter Jim Cohn and I stopped in Atlanta on our way to Augusta and saw the Braves against the Cubs on a Sunday afternoon. Maddux mowed down the woeful Cubbies on that afternoon in record time.

In the evening, Phil Richards and Stan Sutton get in from writing their newspaper articles for their papers in Indy and Louisville. They are both great guys who I love to sit around and talk with every year during our stay in Augusta. Phil wrote for the *South Bend Tribune* in the early 1980s. He has tremendous respect for the *Tribune* Sports Department and how much they cover with the staff size they have. Phil is very organized and neat. Every year he gets the ironing board out and irons his underwear. Besides covering golf, Stan also is the beat writer for the *Louisvlle Courier* on IU basketball. Stan doesn't iron his underwear. Being an IU alum, Mike has several questions for Stan about the Hoo-siers. The four of us watch the endless stream of special shows on The Masters on TV. The Golf Channel airs half-hour shows on Nicklaus' dramatic 1986 Masters championship. They also have a half-hour inter-view with Tiger on his 1997 domination of Augusta National. The local stations do prime time specials. At 10:00 Stan and Phil stay up to watch a special on Fuzzy's 1979 Masters triumph. I'm pooped and konk out. During the course of a day at Augusta National, I'll walk several miles up and down the big hills covering stories. My feet are worn out by the evening. It usually takes me about 10 seconds to fall asleep.

Wednesday April 8

We're back at Augusta National at the crack of dawn. With the gallery still lined up outside, Mike and I go to various scenic locations on the course to do our "stand ups." Mike shoots mine. I then get the camera and shoot for him. It gives a "team coverage" feeling.

By 7:30 AM we're back near the driving range in search of interviews. Nineteen-ninety-seven British Open and 1998 Players Championship winner Justin Leonard emerges from the range. He looks busy but I ask him for an interview anyway. Leonard reluctantly agrees. It's not that he's being a jerk. He simply has a practice round time and he doesn't have much time. His answers are terse and short and I keep the interview to three questions. Like everyone else I've talked to, he doesn't think Augusta National should make drastic course changes just because Tiger manhandled it in 1997. Moments later, one of the true gentlemen and historians of golf walks by us. Gentle Ben Crenshaw is also in a hurry, but obliges us a quick interview. I ask him about the new Notre Dame golf course he and his company are designing off Douglas Road in South Bend. "It's a traditional golf course," Crenshaw says with a smile. "It's kind of old style, old timey routing that you can walk very easily. That's what we concentrated on heavily. We've been honored to do the course."

Knowing Crenshaw is in a hurry, I ask him just that question. I know the WSBT viewers will want to hear about the Notre Dame course. Crenshaw's answer gets me excited about playing it when it is finished.

ESPN's Jimmy Roberts is standing near us. Roberts and his crew do an excellent job of covering golf for SportsCenter. I interview Roberts about his favorites. He picks John Huston as his darkhorse.

After editing our work and uplinking it back to WSBT, Mike and I walk over to the Par 3 course at Augusta National. It's beauty will knock your socks off. Tucked away behind the 10th hole tee box, it is maintained by the same standards that hold to the main golf course. Thousands flock to it to watch the annual Par 3 contest. I give Mike a quick tour of the layout. Along the way we stop and watch Nick Price and Greg Norman. After putting out on the third hole, Norman waits for Fuzzy and John Daly to hit onto the green. As soon as their balls land, Norman knocks the balls into the water. Fuzzy playfully throws up his arms in disbelief. An Augusta National official scurries to mark where the balls landed.

The Par 3 is played for fun. The winner does get a crystal chalice, but mostly it's for fun and to entertain the gallery. Many of the golfers use their children as caddies. In 1997, Corey Pavin had David Robinson of the Spurs as his caddy. The gallery cracked up because of their height difference. Robinson often held the putter high and made little Corey hop up and grab it.

Halfway through the Par 3, storms arrive and the event is called off. Sandy Lyle was leading and is declared the winner. Knowing the traffic will be awful as folks try to exit Augusta National, Mike and I pop into the satellite truck to kill some time. The most recent *Sports Illustrated* is inside, so I plow into that while Mike tries to get his beloved Cubs on WGN. "Argh," he says as he sees their game against the evil Mets is also rained out.

After an hour we say goodbye to the guys in the satellite truck and head back to the house. This is our last day on the course. For the past two years I've just covered the practice rounds Monday, Tuesday, and Wednesday to get features. I end up back home by Thursday afternoon. That's fine with me. I was here for a solid week for the 1994, 1995, and 1996 Masters. With two young children and a wife back at home, I don't like long periods of travel. Besides, The Masters is much better to watch on TV over the weekend than to view in person. CBS does an outstanding job of coverage. As we drive out the parking lot I take one last look back. Over the years I think I've walked over just about every blade of grass there. I've connected to it. People often ask me if I've ever played Augusta National. I haven't, although I could sign up for the chance to play it. They pick a certain amount of media members to play it the day after the tournament. The holes are left from where they were on the final round on Sunday. Being a semi-hacker, I'd make a fool out of myself. No kidding, I would five-putt many greens because they're so treacherous. I would probably shoot a 110 when normally I shoot an 88. They'd probably ask me to leave or sign something saying I'd never attempt to play it again.

APRIL
Friday
10

Helping Inner-City Teens
at the Ray Bird Ministries

Having traveled back from Augusta to South Bend on Thursday, I'm back at WSBT at 12:30 Friday afternoon to tape a "Making A Difference" feature. Laurent, our peppy news photographer from France, is assigned to the shoot. With Laurent chattering a mile a minute, we drive west of South Bend to Bass Lake, sight of the Ray Bird Ministries. We turn off Edison onto a dirt road that winds us up to their 65-acre facility sitting right on the lake.

The Ray Bird Ministries is a Christian organization dedicated since 1920 to reaching out to at-risk children and teens. Their mission is to share the gospel of Jesus Christ with at-risk children of the Michiana area through community and camp ministries.

Terry Lang, who's in charge of the teen program, greets us and tells us about the theme of this particular week. It's for teens to "Passionately Pursue Purity." It's Spring Break week for area schools, so there are a lot of teens on the grounds. "We tell them to passionately pursue purity," Terry tells me. "We believe teens in this generation need to learn what courtship is rather than just going out and dating. Dating is a very selfish thing; look at that person and look at what 'I' can get from that relationship. Courtship says I'll wait until I'm mature enough and ready enough and committed enough to make proper relationships that will be lifelong relationships and not just some short-term gratification that eventually sets up a dynamic that they fail again and again."

Terry takes us upstairs in the main building where the at-risk teens are singing songs about Christ. "Kids come here with a lot of emotional baggage," he says as we stand in the back of the room. "We see a lot of healing here, kids working through issues in their lives. We also believe in process. People don't change overnight and you need people to walk with you over the long haul, and we're here for the long haul."

There are weekly Bible studies and fellowships for the kids throughout the year. They're also involved in special work projects, adventure trips, and all sorts of events throughout the year. The summer is when Ray Bird Ministries is busiest, with over 600 children from at-risk neighborhoods in Michiana. "When the kids fail, we say that God gives second chances," Terry says. "Eventually they grab a hold of some good truths and character. We teach them how to serve their communities. The hope for a lot of the inner city teens is Jesus Christ. He comes in and makes a big difference in their lives. We also see a lot that if they don't grab a hold of the spiritual aspect, they learn to become more solid citizens in the community."

After singing, the teens spill out onto the grounds and start on their various work projects. I pick a few kids out of the blue and ask them about their experience. One youngster tells me that by reading his Bible regularly he is learning how to live his life. Another tells me of his personal relationship with Christ. Both are kids who obviously have big-time obstacles in their home life. Without being a part of the Ray Bird Ministries, they could have easily been swallowed into a path of hopelessness.

Many people have heard of the Ray Bird Ministries or been connected to them in some way over the years. But as we're about to leave, Terry tells me in some ways they're a hidden diamond west of town. That's not right. More people should know about their effective ministries.

There are two things they need:

    (1) Financial support—they are on a shoestring budget.

    (2) Volunteers to help work with the teens and to do handywork on the grounds.

Here's the number if you would like to help them make a difference: (219) 232-8523.

In the evening, between the 6:00 and 10:00 newscasts, I edit the feature to run this coming Tuesday. I won't see it air on the news that particular night. Jack and I are headed to Mississippi for our annual fishing trip with Jack's grandad. Our journey to the cotton fields of Mississippi will also give me a chance to spend time with my grandfather, who just happened to turn 101 years old!

APRIL
Monday
13

Heading to Mississippi

Five-year-old Jack and I are headed south to visit my dad (Jack's granddad) and my granpapa in the Delta of Mississippi. We had planned on driving part of the way Sunday evening, but, as usual, I got caught up in watching the final round of The Masters on CBS. Jack and I have gone down each year to go fishing with Grandad. Little Abby will probably start going next year, but at two and a half she's not the patient sort to wait calmly for the bobber to go under the water.

The drive south takes all day. As the sun sets, co-pilot Jack and I zip by Memphis. By my estimation, Jack has asked 2,242 questions to this point.

"How many tires are on a big long truck?"

"How do they build bridges?"

"Are we in Mississippi yet?" (I started getting this question just south of Rochester, Indiana.)

"Does Grandad still take long naps?"

"Can we stop at a toy store? I promise I'll just look. . ."

Darkness settles in as we pass Mississippi towns like Senatobia, Batesville, and Grenada. We drive by Greenwood and then start hitting the back roads of the Delta, which has some of the richest farm soil in the world. We go through Sidon and cross bridges like the one in "Ode to Billy Joe."

Wearily, 14 hours after leaving South Bend, we pull into tiny Morgan City. With a population of about 200 it takes me about 30 seconds to drive through Morgan City and get to the cozy, modest white house that I've been visiting my entire 36 years.

The screen door opens as my father greets us in the driveway. Dad has lived there since the early 1990s, primarily to care for my grandparents as they went well into their 90s. He's there by himself these days. Gram passed away at age 93. Granpapa is up the road in Greenwood in a nursing home still going strong at 101. Memories of Gram greeting me with a warm hug rush over me as we walk through the screen porch into the kitchen. In years past, a quick glance at the oven (as she said, "Ohhhh, so good to see you!") would always reveal fried okra, country ham with red eyed gravy, butter beans, black eyed peas, fried chicken, and cornbread. The hot biscuits were being kept warm inside the oven so they could be buttered just right. Granpapa was always out in the garden when I arrived for those visits. After greeting Gram, I would always go back outside to their big backyard and walk past the mighty magnolia shade trees as the screen door closed with a loud pop behind me. I always found Granpapa in his tan pants and shirt and thatchy hat hard at work in his garden, oblivious to what was going on outside the rows of tilled soil. More times than not I found him tending to his 'maters, as folks down south often call tomatoes. We'd talk for a few minutes. I'd have to raise my voice because, for as long as I can remember, he was a bit hard of hearing. Thank goodness I always had a "TV News" voice. Rarely did I have to repeat things. On this cool April night, Dad's warmed-up supper doesn't meet Gram's standards, but "it'll do" as some of my relatives like to say.

We stay up and talk mainly about the trip down from Indiana. People in Mississippi are known to ask dozens of questions about what roads you took on a trip and what kind of time you made. If you make good time on a long trip by "only getting out of the car to go to the bathroom, get gas, and a quick bite to eat," then you are viewed as a conquering road champion.

After putting Jack to bed, Dad and I sit up and talk a little longer. He's got one of those Direct TV deals so I take the opportunity to put on The Golf Channel. I still can't believe they do nightly half hour newscasts solely on golf news of the day. In the morning, we'll make the drive into Greenwood to talk with a man born in 1897, my grandfather Everett Adams, Sr.

APRIL
Tuesday
14

Reflections from My
101-Year-Old Grandfather

After a country breakfast and a look at the sports section of the *Jackson Clarion-Ledger* newspaper, the three of us get in my car and drive back 20 miles towards Greenwood to visit Granpapa. As we pull into the Golden Age Nursing Home parking lot, Dad informs me how he always parks his car *right next* to the entrance because he comes there just about every day (even though cars are not supposed to be parked there). He would park inside the nursing home and inside Granpapa's room if he could get away with it. I've known him to circle grocery story parking lots for 10 minutes to get the closest spot. Heck, his church in Morgan City is *one* block away from his house and he DRIVES to church!

"There sure are a lot of grandads in here," Jack says as we walk through the nursing home.

Granpapa is sitting up as we enter his room. He is plowing through lunch. His voracious appetite, which I inherited, is still going strong.

"Daddy," my dad says, "Charlie and Jack are here."

Granpapa smiles and reaches out with a warm handshake. He can't see worth a lick and the hearing's about gone, too, but his mind is still sharp.

"How's Notre Dame going to do this year?" he asks me as I sit down. "As a kid growing up we all used to hear about Notre Dame football."

Everett Louis Adams was born in Zama, Mississippi, in 1897. He grew up outside Ethel, Mississippi (who was in charge of naming those tiny towns anyway?), on a large farm his daddy owned. They went to church in an ox wagon with oxen named "Rock" and "Raleigh."

"I went to a one-teacher school," Granpapa reflected to his daughter Dorothy Hubbard some years ago. "There were no blackboards, just the walls painted black. The teacher didn't have a college education. He just felt a calling to teach and said, 'I'm a teacher.' The schools were in levels, not grades—Primary level, Intermediate level, and 'the rest of them.' The adjoining community to ours had a two-teacher school, so my father let me ride a mule six miles to it. The school was just 9th, 10th, and 11th grade. Its curriculum didn't have enough for a diploma. The principal gave me a certificate [a note that said Everett was a "well-schooled young man"] after the 11th grade and I packed up and went to Mississippi College with $25 in my pocket. I went to the Registrar and he took a long hard long at the certificate. You would have thought he was reading a death message. He finally looked up and said, 'Mr. Adams, you don't have anything to enter college on. We'll give you a trial. If you make it, you can stay. If not...' I carried every subject except math, which I dropped. I'd never had anything except Algebra 1. You've got to have a sound foundation in math when you get to classes like Theory of Equations. I spent $130 for my entire freshman year, including tuition, board, food, books, and train fare.

"After a little college, World War I started and there was a crying need for teachers. I was a very sickly young man growing up, never weighed over 118 pounds despite being 5' 11." I didn't get accepted in the military. The country was advertising for teachers. I saw one and answered it. I felt I needed to serve the country any way I could. I took the State Teachers exam in Mississippi and passed it. Soon afterwards I got a letter from a school in South Carolina saying I'd been elected principal there. I'd never even taught a class at that point. Well, folks in my own community were looking for principals, so I wrote the South Carolina people and declined. I became principal of a two-teacher school in Holmes County making $75 a month. Before long, a superintendent made me principal/teacher of a five-teacher school in Bethesda. It had some sharp students. I often stayed up until midnight studying the lesson plans so that I could give them the quality teaching they deserved.

I took them to the Literary Academy Competition in the big city. The big schools were labeled 'A' and little consolidated schools like us were labeled 'B.' We scored more points than all the rest of the students in the 'B' schools put together. I hope I'm not trying to throw a bouquet at myself. It just shows how bright these particular students were. One would go on to become the governor of Tennessee: Buford Ellington."

Along the way, Granpapa developed a love for baseball. It was far and away his favorite sport. Over the years his favorites were Grover Cleveland Alexander, Walter "Big Train" Johnson, Dizzy Dean, Honus Wagner, Ty Cobb, and Ted Williams. The Phillies have always been his favorite team.

He married Ruth Riley at 9:30 in the morning of August 16, 1921. They had wanted to get married for a long time, but it took them six years to have enough money to start a life together. The regular Presbyterian ministers were out of town on their wedding day, so the Reverend W.A. Bowling, a Methodist circuit preacher, married them. He goofed up and pronounced them "Mr. and Mrs. E.L. Blanton.'" Ruth's brother, Dick, "punched" the Reverend and said, "No, you're wrong about that!" They married so early in the day because there plans were to catch the train for New Orleans for their honeymoon. They missed it and ended up going to the old Durant Hotel instead.

They would go on to be married for 72 years.

Granpapa ended up being a teacher, principal, and/or superintendent for 42 years. The highest salary he ever made was $6,000 a year at Itta Bena High School. He also worked part time at the Cotton Gin in Sidon that year. He and Gram raised six children (chil'un, as they say down south), three girls and three boys.

Granpapa was a principal/teacher at several schools. With a wife and six children, there was the responsibility of food and clothes.

"After the school year I would work the summers for extra income. I used the kayser blade on the highways, I would hew cross ties, work at the saw mill or be a bookkeeper at the cotton gin. Whatever I could get to give us something to live on. Along the way I kept going to college when I could to work on my degree. Finally finished it up at the University of Southern Mississippi. I did some basketball coaching along the way. The only sports that rural schools had were boys' and girls' basketball. If your team got its name in the newspaper enough, the big schools would call you to play them. I ordered books on coaching, but learned coaching is more instinct than book learning. In coaching, you survey your team and its strengths and you survey the opposing team and its strengths. You go from there."

To satisfy his keen interest in sports, he bought a grandiose new Atwater-Kent cabinet radio on fancy legs. At night he would press his ear against it to listen to Babe Ruth and all the greats play ball. His wife Ruth gave him a hard time over that purchase. They couldn't afford it (she just didn't understand what it means to be a sports nut!). Despite that squabble, their 72 years of marriage were built on love and respect for one another.

"Ruth was 'the best.' She was loveable, efficient, and far-seeing. She had all the plusses when it came to being a first-class person. For our children, she more than made up for the weaknesses I had."

Ruth Riley was a true lady with a fierce pride in herself and her beloved family; she had a fine instinct for the best people (not necessarily the richest or the most prominent—but the best). She was quick to recognize when a person was in the process of fulfilling their responsibility in life, and she responded in kind. She was always sure that better days were just around the corner. Her faith never flagged—in God, her Church, and in her family. They moved many times while Granpapa was in search of a better job. Raising six kids that way is tough, but she persevered. Since most of the schools Granpapa worked at were rural schools, there was no running water or indoor plumbing. It was tough, but Ruth could laugh, and often did. However, when their son Bill died years later, that laughter was harder to come by. That was the most searing experience of her life. Her daughter Dorothy remembers once asking her, "Mother, after Bill's death, what was the most disappointing experience of your life?" Just as quick as a flash, with no pondering whatsoever, she said, "The divorces in the family." When she came along, divorce was *never* an option for solving problems.

The four decades Granpapa spent in Education as a principal and teacher left these impressions:

"I never had any trouble with discipline. Boys and girls, if they realize they're getting a fair deal, they're easy to get along with. I never had a bit of trouble. The way to control children is make them realize they're getting something worthwhile and that you'd love to be their buddy. If you treat them right, I think they play the game 50-50. The worst mistake we can make with young folks is let them get the impression that we think they don't know anything themselves—that we've got to lord it over to them."

Being a principal at several schools was testing.

"I reckon I shouldn't say it, but boards of trustees and people like that, they enter politics too and sometimes teachers are chosen so that they'll get so-and-so the most votes in the next election. You may not agree with that, but it's my opinion. Teachers should be selected based on academics first."

Of their six children, he felt Bill Adams was the tops in education.

"I had taught him in grammar school and promoted him to high school because of his ability, not his age. When he went to the high school, it was upstairs. They stopped him and at first said, 'you belong downstairs.' He was a little fella. When it came time to pick the valedictorian, they finally gave it to Betty Crawley. Objections were raised quickly. Do you know who raised them? Betty did. She said 'I've been in this class with Bill for four years and he's by far the smartest student and should be valedictorian.'"

I've always been amazed at how much food Granpapa can eat. I've been 6' 5" and well over 200 pounds for many years and he and his rail thin 5' 11" frame have always put me to shame at the supper table. As my cousin Bill Hubbard says, "He can eat enough to choke a horse." Cornbread and sweet milk has always been a favorite. And, yes, he has eaten a whole bunch of bacon and sausage in his 101 years.

Gram lived to be 93. "There's a blank here, a void in my life that just can't be replaced."

On March 26, 1998 Granpapa turned 101. Their nephew Bill Hubbard, I thought, hit their longevity right on the head with this observation: "I don't think you get to those ages without letting an awful lot of life's problems run off like water on a duck's back. Sure, when things don't go like you would have them go, it makes you wonder how you could've made it different, but you don't let anything consume you and forever take away what good there is in life."

Granpapa died in the evening on September 2, 1998 of pneumonia. Among those paying their respects at his visitation and funeral were students of his from the 1920s. Well into their 80s, they came to the funeral home in Greenwood to share the impact he had on their lives as a principal and teacher 70 years ago. Everett Louis Adams, Sr., was buried next to his wife Ruth in Kosiesko, Mississippi. He was 101 years old.

APRIL
Thursday
16

Coming Back Home

It's time for Jack and I to head back to Indiana. On our way back we stop in my hometown of Oxford, Mississippi, to visit my sister, who is at Ole Miss, and my cousins Barbara Lowe Moen and Richard Lowe. Amanda is a big Ole Miss basketball fan who is still trying to cope with Bryce Drew's last second shot that knocked them out of the NCAA's. I try to comfort her by telling her what a great guy Bryce is and that he comes from a wonderful family. "If some outlaw basketball program with a thug that never went to class had beat us with a shot like that, it would be unbearable," I tell her. "But at least we can take solace in that Bryce Drew slew us. Stabbing that Bryce Drew doll relentlessly at night in your dorm will only make things worse."

Jack and I leave Oxford after lunch with Nashville as our stopping-point goal. Jack wants a hotel with an indoor pool. Sounds good, but as we get past Jackson, Tennessee, going east on the interstate all the radio stations break in with reports of tornadoes *in* downtown Nashville. "I do believe we'll be stopping before we get to Nashville," I tell myself. We find a place about 30 miles out. After swimming for a while, we settle into the room and watch the Nashville stations coverage of the tornadoes.

Ironically, I would come to learn later that former Notre Dame coach

Lou Holtz of CBS Sports happened to be in Nashville at the time and was flying back to their home in Orlando. Lou never got used to the frigid weather in South Bend. "There's nothing south about South Bend," he would often say. There's warmth in Orlando, as well as adventurous weather. "I'm writing a book about the things they didn't tell me when we moved to Orlando," Holtz joked. "Like, it's the lightning capital of the world!"

APRIL
Monday
20

Getting Roasted Alive

Back on February 15th I got a letter at WSBT from Jack Colwell of the *South Bend Tribune:*

> *Dear Charlie: As headtable chairman for the 1998 South Bend Press Club Gridiron Show, I would like to invite you to be our guest at the headtable for the April 20th production at the University of Notre Dame's Joyce Center.*

Oh oh. That's a nice way of saying I'm going to get ROASTED! I'm going to be ridiculed by the roastmasters as a spotlight shines on me! Sounds like fun.

Actually, I was roasted at the Gridiron Show in 1994 alongside Clay's State Championship coach Tom DeBaets, Notre Dame's basketball star Monty Williams, and many others from the local news and business scene. I know the drill. I can take it!!

The first order of business is to go get a tux. Weary of cumber buns or however you spell them, I go with a snazzy looking vest this year. Fits much better.

Sherrad and I get to the Notre Dame Monogram Room at 5:30 for the pre-Roast reception. South Bend Chocolate Company owner Mark

Tarner arrives with wife Julie to get verbally scarred also. The program says that "Mark first launched his business at 3300 W. Sample St in 1991 and that he actually remodeled the building. That was the first change in the West Side since Caparell's got painted in 1980."

All of us get zinged. Michigan City mayor Sheila Brillson is "applauded" in the program for "having a big year with casinos floating into town. On a clear day, you can see the polyester aura hanging over Michigan City from all the seniors who now regard the city by the lake as their second home. Let the dice roll. Grandma needs a new part of orthopedics."

At the head table, I sit next to State Senator Cleo Washington. He, Mayor Steve Luecke, and St. Joseph County prosecutor Mike Barnes, and I talk about Notre Dame football and the NCAA Tournament. The program declares that "Barnes serves on the National District Attorneys Association and periodically meets with Janet Reno. At those meetings, he usually gives her fashion advice."

As for me, it's told that the Big Board Sports I do is actually "Big *Bored* Sports." I just smile as I stand there and take it.

Penn High football coach Chris Geesman, we're "told," looked into taking the Notre Dame football coaching job "but didn't want to leave Penn for a smaller school."

Tribune sportswriting gem David Haugh is lauded for covering Notre Dame football. "Sometimes that's a trip to Ireland and sometimes that's a trip to West Lafayette."

One of the highlights of the evening is listening to Sharon McGovern play the piano. I have always been an admirer of those who play the piano. My mother tried to get me to stay with it, but baseball gloves and bats pulled me away. I can, to this day, play Kum Ba Yah (is that how you spell it?). The singing and dancing performances are quite a show. WSBT's Robert "vertically challenged" Borrelli comes across like a young Fred Astaire. Smith Barney's Craig Blue does a striking impersonation of President Bill Clinton. By the way, Craig can make you a small fortune. But you have to give him a large fortune to start with . . .

Patty Thornton happens to be the assistant chairman of the Press Club this year. The program informs us that "she is the TV traffic manager at WSBT. That means Patty arranges commercials. She is the one who allows commercials to be broadcast even though the store's sale was over days ago."

Kathy Borlik is the Grid Show chairman for this particular year. At the podium she looks at all of us in our snazzy tuxes and evening dresses. "I got my evening wear from the large and lumpy section at Target," Kathy says.

I am thoroughly entertained during the evening. The writing is very funny. The skits are well rehearsed and executed (I am EXECUTED verbally at the head table!). My wife has a great time sitting at the WSBT table with such assorted nuts as Raphael Morton, Debra Daniel, Meg Sauer, and Jonathon (Chia Pet) Miller.

The Press Club annual show is heading into its 50th year in 1999. It's a hoot! Check it out. Call the Tribune at 235-6161 if you'd like to get tickets.

A Motivational Talk
to High School Students

This is an important day to me. It's a chance to help touch the lives of some outstanding young folks and hopefully help guide them as they take their gifts and abilities out into "the world." A few months ago, Edwardsburg High School guidance counselor Sally Dalrymple invited me to be the guest speaker at the induction ceremony of the Edwardsburg Chapter of the National Honor Society. I gladly accept because I feel I have some things to share that are candid yet important for these teens, and all teens, to hear (and re-hear). In my head I always have an outline of the talk I give to teens. But before every talk, including this one, I start working on it three to four days before the speech. I jot down the most important points and then over the next few days add to it with timely and topical events.

This morning, I drive to Scottsdale Mall to return my rented tux from Monday's South Bend Press Club Roast. I then go upstairs to the mall's food area and sit down at an isolated table with my briefcase and notes. For an hour I go over every part of my talk and try to weave in humor as well as very serious parts. I fret that I'll come across too stern, but these are important topics. Eventually, I stop preparing and leave the rest up to Faith—that certain things will come to me during the speech. It's somewhat scary, yet exciting to know that ideas just pop up during the actual talk.

As I head north on Highway 23 through Granger and into M-62 in Michigan, I play parts of the speech over and over in my head. I practice my opening jokes several times because I don't have rhythm when it comes to telling jokes. Bob Nagle, Mayor Robert Beutter, and J.T. in the Morning can flat out tell jokes. For me, I grope along hoping not to screw up the punchline.

I get to Edwardsburg an hour early and pull into a restaurant to do some last minute revisions. As I walk in, town folk do a double take. "What's Charlie doing here during the news hour?" is racing through their minds. It's pretty funny. After going through the notes with my chicken sandwich, I make the short drive to Edwardsburg middle school. It's the speech sight because, like many middle schools, it has a swankier auditorium than the high school. It's still an hour before the ceremony. Sally greets me in the hall way. Seeing she's busy, I wander through the building for one more run-through. At the far end of a hallway is the French class room. For 30 minutes, I wander through Paris as I add and delete from my notes for the final time.

I'm so impressed with the National Honor Society students I meet before the ceremony. President Elizabeth Newell tells me she's very nervous about all the speaking she will have to do, but as the program starts she reads from the podium like a professional speaker. Assistant Superintendent Anthony Koontz addresses the audience about **leadership**. He gives several definitions of leadership: "Leadership is not a right—but a responsibility. Real leaders are ordinary people with extraordinary determination." —Thomas Jefferson. "Any leader takes people where they want to go. A *great* leader takes people where they don't necessarily want to go, but ought to be."—Henry Ford. "Leaders get out in front and stay there by raising the standards by which they judge themselves—and by which they are willing to be judged." —Benjamin Franklin. "The only place success comes before work is in the dictionary."—Lee Iacoca. Anthony concludes his talk on leadership by encouraging the inductees to "be an ordinary individual with extraordinary determination."

Annette Cloud, Jennifer Gans, David Root, and Christine Vint grace the room with instrumental music. They're followed by vocal music from Stacey LaPlace, Karie McGowan, Rebecca Meuninck, Alison Mikulyuk, and Kate Schildhouse. Elizabeth then gives a very polished introduction

of me and up to the podium I stride. I fire off a couple of jokes that elicit laughs. I incorporate Edwardsburg High principal David Zech in one, much to his surprise. David came to Edwardsburg after many fine years as principal at River Valley High School.

With the young people respectfully giving me their attention, I shift gears to the serious mode. I tell them that I'm 35 years old. I don't have the wisdom of someone in their 70s, but am at a point in life where I have a very firm grasp of what works and what doesn't work as far as contentment and happiness in life. Through the mistakes and successes I have made, and all that I've learned from the hundreds of high profile coaches, athletes, and community newsmakers over the years, I feel very secure that what I am about to tell them will help guide them down the right path.

My first point of emphasis is on how they can truly *be happy and content in life*. I'm sure many of them are aware of this because it is part of the foundation of the National Honor Society. I'm talk about serving others. I tell them that the happiness and satisfaction I draw from my broadcasting profession is certainly not from getting my pea head mug on TV, but by doing stories that recognize deserving people and organizations in our community. I tell them how happy it makes me to do a "Making a Difference" story on an inner-city tutoring program that needs computers and learn that the next day a business that viewed the story immediately bought them the computers they needed. A wonderful example of someone whose life has been built around serving others from a media view is Bill Moor of the *South Bend Tribune*. He's humble and doesn't draw attention to himself, but throughout his writing career he has done hundreds of inspirational stories that have brightened the lives of many. There's no telling how many folks have his columns framed in their homes. No doubt, that's led to a warm feeling inside him, though I'm sure he has always taken the attitude that he has just done the job the *Tribune* wants him to do. That's serving others. I encourage them to pursue a path in life that is built around helping others with the intelligience and gifts they've been blessed to have. I urge them not to fall into the trap Madison Avenue delivers in advertising that proclaims a "me, me, me" world.

From there I warn them to not have a love OF **money**. I tell them of a recent survey revealing that 80% of pro athletes are divorced within two years after ending their athletic careers. That shows their marriages were built, in many cases, on those big paychecks that come in during the short span of a professional athlete. I tell them that to beware if their future endeavors are planned in the hopes of making "lots of money." 1st Timothy reads, "Those who want to become rich bring temptation to themselves and are caught in a trap. The love of money causes all kinds of evil." I tell them that many pro athletes and other successful make a lot of money, but generously share it with worthy causes. They stay away from a love OF money. God loves a cheerful giver, especially those that don't draw attention to what they give. There are many successful business persons in the area that give heartily and the average Joe on the street never reads about it in the paper.

Knowing that these high school juniors and seniors are about to embark on careers, I tell them that one of the biggest decisions they'll make in life is **what they do for their career**. Don't fall into the trap of picking something that is impressive to others. It might be something that bores your socks off. In my case, local TV news sportscasting provides an unbelievable challenge every day. It can be exciting. It can serve others and it gives me a good feeling of accomplishment when I drive home every day. Sure, it can have drudgery. Sometimes I sit at my computer writing scripts and ordering credentials and all sorts of office work. But, all in all, it's a never ending adventure. My hope is that these teens will do things like enter the Education field and take jobs in the most challenging areas. That they'll realize that God will provide them with their daily bread and they don't need snazzy cars and huge closets full of clothes. I tell them of John Grisham's book, *The Street Lawyer* (which I mentioned earlier in this book) and how that could help inspire them.

From there I move on to **decisions.** Driving into Edwardsburg, I saw a billboard with the picture of an attractive young lady. It read, "Sex Can Wait. I'm Worth the Wait." I tell them of the story of former professional boxer Tommy Morrison, who fought in championship fights and was in a *Rocky* movie. In 1996 he tested HIV positive. At a news conference he said: "To all my young fans, I'd ask that you no longer see me as a role model, but as an individual that had the opportunity to be a role model and blew it-blew it with irresponsible, irrational, and immature decisions. Decisions that could one day cost me my life. I thought I was bullet proof. I'm not."

I tell them of what I recently saw at the Ray Bird Ministries. How the young people there were being taught to "Passionately Pursue Purity." I tell them of A.C. Green of the Dallas Mavericks NBA team. The November 17, 1997, issue of *Sports Illustrated* had a story on Green about how at age 35 he is still a virgin. In the article, Green tells writer Michael Farber, "I am curious (about sex). But not curious enough to go to the violation point. I figure God created it, so it must be good. But He has created it to take place at a certain point of time—within the confines of marriage. If I'm going to live according to rules God laid out, then there are rules A through Z. There can't be situational ethics." I wish I could say that I was a virgin before marriage, but when I got away from the Word after high school it wasn't long before I was down the path of premarital sexual sin. Oh, the hollowness that came from that. But God's grace and the tugging of the Holy Spirit led me away from that lifestyle. I truly repented and asked and received forgiveness. "But if we confess our sins, he will forgive our sins, because we can trust God to do what is right. He will cleanse us from all the wrong things we have done." That's from 1st John. There certainly has to be complete repentance following the forgiveness. Yes, I have remorse about it, but I no longer beat myself up about it. God means it when He says He forgives. We don't get extra credit if we punish ourselves mentally for years.

I urge them to take caution about the decisions they make regarding alcohol. Since I've never been stupid enough to even try a drug, I always forget to rail on that danger. It boggles my mind that someone would be dumb enough to get into drugs. I've screwed up in the past, but I never had any trouble telling someone selling drugs to get lost. Usually, they detected my attitude about it and never bothered approaching me.

I tell the students all of this boils down to **who you spend time with** in the future. When I was in high school, I was constantly around my Christian friends. When I got into college and professional lives, I started spending some time with folks that were good guys on the surface, but morally questionable inside. The very first thing a young person should do upon getting to college or a town where they're starting work is to connect with a church body of their faith. The Bible should be their guiding light. "The orders of the Lord are right. They make people happy. The commands of the Lord are pure—they light up the way." That's from Psalm 19:8-11. Young people have to have their spiritual armor on or they will take hits. "How can a young person live a pure life? By obeying your Word." Psalm 119:9.

My next point of emphasis is **attitude**. I urge them not to dwell on the negatives that will come up in their life. That will eat them up. They will find themselves around moaners, groaners, and complainers who will want to bring them down to their grumpy level. I tell them that their attitude will dictate in may ways how happy or downtrodden they become in life. The key is to see the good in others. They'll encounter bosses and co-workers who have all sorts of warts. Find the good in those characters. Cling to it. I ask them to remember to have balance in their lives as they get established in a career one day. When I was a young sportscaster, I was "work, work, work" and not much else. That's not right. They need to be careful about who they work for down the road. Many bosses feel outworking the competition leads to success. They constantly call in workers on their days off. I constantly make sure Matt Burridge has his two days off. If he has to come in on one of them, he gets a COMP day off very soon. Same with Mike Stack. I'm sure all these folks who have busted their tails for corporations for years only to find they had to be laid off are still wondering what the heck happened. I implore them to remain active in fitness or to start getting involved in exercise. I work out just about every day. I need the energy that comes from exercise. Without it, I become Blah Man. There's not many better feelings than making it through a 10K race and celebrating with everyone else who has fought to complete the 6.2 miles.

In conclusion, I urge these young people to know what they stand for professional and personally. Professionally, I stand for local sports coverage with an emphasis on the positive. Some folks have a problem with that, but at least they know where I'm coming from. Whenever I come across someone in *local* news that thinks we should do more *national* coverage, my little "is that person a Communist?" antennae goes up.

Personally, I stand for Jesus Christ as my Lord and Savior. That pretty much takes care of my stand and foundation.

I ask them to be people of integrity and character. I stumbled in that area as a young person, breaking my contract with WTOK-TV in

Meridian, Mississippi, to take an offer in California. Again, those days I made many decisions without proper thought, prayer, and guidance. That was wrong. On the day I'm giving this speech, Green Bay's Reggie White changes his mind about retiring and returns to the Packers for one last season. He explains how he had promised the Packers he would play this season and that he was a man of his word. He felt it was wrong to retire even if his back was giving him all sorts of problems at age 36.

As I wind down I rehit on some points. I tell them that looking back to their age, I wish I had known the Bible better and that would have led to better decisions. I tell them how the Bible says not to worry about anything, but to pray and ask God about everything they need, always giving thanks. My talk goes for about 20 minutes. Afterwards, 38 students are inducted into the National Honor Society. They recite the Pledge: "I pledge myself to uphold the high purposes of the National Honor Society to which I have been selected. Striving in every way by word and deed to make its ideals the ideals of my school and of my life." Principal David Zech congratulates all the inductees and gives a special thanks to Sally Dalrymple for her dedication in the National Honor Society and as a guidance counselor. Sally's retiring after this school year.

There's a reception after the induction ceremony where I get to meet many of the parents who were in attendance. I am so impressed with the people of the Edwardsburg community. To me, it's very exciting to think about what these talented and hard working young people are going to do down the road. Much of the credit will go to their fine high school. All high schools should model their football stadium and press box after Leo Hoffman Field. It is first-rate. Go Eddies!

APRIL
Thursday
23

A Visit to Rotary

Over the years I've had the opportunity to speak to many of the civic organizations that add so much to our community. Back in February, Bob Prevette of the Roseland Rotary Club asked me to speak to its group on this date in April. It meets each Thursday at the St. Mary's Main Dining Hall. No, they don't get to eat lunch with all the young ladies of St. Mary's. If that were the case, their membership would probably overflow. Instead, they're given a nice room underneath the Main Dining Hall. The Roseland Rotary Club was founded in 1968. A charter member was the president of St. Mary's who willed that the club could meet at the college as long as its members wanted. I love going to luncheons of Rotary and Kiwanis Clubs, big or small. The Pledge of Allegiance to the Flag and the invocation at the start warms my heart. The members always zing each other with razor sharp wit, but the bottom line is they come together to serve God, country, and community. The men and women of the Roseland Rotary Club have accomplished all sorts of positive things in the community—Food Basket Programs, Salvation Army work, scholarships for high school seniors, foreign exchange student programs, and much more.

Dave Keck of Keck's Klear Water Company (all natural!) introduces me to the members. Beforehand, as we chow down turkey and mashed potatoes, Dave tells me about his golf game. "They call me Omar because I'm in the sand so much," Dave reveals. I can sympathize. Clay High School senior Kristin Moo is among those at our table. She is part of the Rotary Interact Club through Clay which teaches the ideas of Rotary. "Our teachers at Clay are awesome," Kristin tells me. "There's a friendly atmosphere at Clay." I ask her who her favorite teachers are. "Mr. Dan Kasper and Mrs. Mary Short!"

After Dave's introduction of me (which I wrote for him on scratch paper during lunch), I talk for 15 minutes about sports. Seeing that there's a lot of Notre Dame football fans I emphasize how the Irish look going into the Blue-Gold game and the 1998 season. Over the years I've talked to a lot of civic groups at lunch. The guest speaker generally starts his or her talk around 12:45. Generally, they try to have the program over by 1:15 so they can all get back to work. Years ago, I didn't realize that and would get startled when several people would get up towards the end of my talk and just walk out of the room. "I should jazz up my talks," I'd think to myself. Actually, they were just getting back to work. Colin Powell could have been giving them a talk and they still would have had to get back to the bakery and tend to yeast and such. One neat thing about the Roseland Rotary Club is that if a member has to leave early, they come to the speaker during lunch and let them know. That's a nice gesture.

This evening's Flash Frame on the 6:00 WSBT newscast is Bill Cosby. The usual flood of calls pour into the newsroom, but the first to get through is Mary Mitchell of Buchanan. She wins a valuable football from the Grand Opening of the College Football Hall of Fame back in 1995. "I'm 33 years old and I had never won anything in my life until this," she excitedly tells me on the phone after the newscast. The tickets to the Hall of Fame in her prize package are especially meaningful to her as she plans to take her husband to the highly acclaimed facility the very next day. I ask her if she watches WSBT News regularly. "Yes we do," she answers. "When my son Tyler was a one-year-old baby he used to sit glued by the TV watching Cindy Ward. We've been loyal viewers ever since!" THAT'S what we need to do to ensure future viewers. We should have Dennis Elsbury from WSBT Promotions drive around town and go into houses and plop their babies down in front of the set at 6:00. I'll see if that's workable!

A Notre Dame Football Spring Weekend

The Notre Dame Blue-Gold football game weekend is not so much about the game, but about the events that surround it. The game is usually pretty vanilla since the coaches don't want the season opening opponent to see anything new they've put in. But since the money from the Blue-Gold game goes to scholarships, it's a very important spring tradition. It's also a great opportunity for fans to get autographs from the players and coaches after the game.

The Friday evening before the Blue-Gold intra-squad game always features the Moose Krause Memorial Scholar-Athlete Dinner at St. Hedwig's in South Bend. Moose was a legendary athlete, coach, and athletic director at Notre Dame. The Krause Chapter of the National Football Foundation and College Football Hall of Fame has raised a lot of scholarship dollars over the years that has gone to high school football players all over the area. Most of the kids don't even go to Notre Dame. Many go to DePauw, Ball State, Purdue, and on and on. Currently, the chapter has 11 students attending colleges from Harvard to Berkley. They're all getting partial tuition help from the Moose Krause chapter.

I love going to the dinner at St. Hedwig's. Each year, I always have Matt or Mike do a story on the evening and interview those being honored. This year former Adams football coach Bill Farrell is being honored for his contributions to football. Among other things, Farrell coached former Notre Dame running back Anthony Johnson, who was a key player on the '88 National Champs. Anthony is one of the finest athletes and man of character ever produced in South Bend. Recently, Thom Jeiger in Sales at WSBT approached me and said University Park Mall was looking for some South Bend-produced athletes and coaches to honor in the mall. I strongly suggested Anthony Johnson. "Everybody wants to win, but I don't think that is the only goal we should have," says Farrell. "We want our young men to be involved in this wonderful team sport so they can understand what it means to be a TEAM member. Hopefully, then they will understand what unity means and what it is to make sacrifices. These are the things that will help them in life, on down the road when they face the many problems we all will face."

Penn's Chris Geesman is presented the Gordon Ford Award for Excellence. Gordon was one of the most active members of the Krause chapter for 22 years. He always did more than his share, whether his role was chapter secretary, dinner co-chairman, or ticket seller supreme. "Gordon would do anything for the club," Chapter president Bill Starck III says. "We'd say 'can you do this?' and he did it!"

As always, Bob Nagle is the emcee. Bob says he has been trying to lose seven pounds so that he can get into some of big Brian Boulac's old clothes.

Several of the scholar-athletes on hand receive scholarship money that they will use in college. LaPorte's Benjamin Dames is the top scholar-athlete. Dames is #1 in the senior class at LaPorte with a 4.1 GPA. Standing 5' 9," 165 pounds, he started games at halfback, flanker, linebacker, and defensive back as well as playing special teams for Coach Bob Schellinger. "He will play anywhere and do anything to help the team," says Schellinger. "He is a great example of what a high school athlete should be."

There are 10 Scholar-Athletes all together, including guard/linebacker Neil Durban of Marian (4.1 GPA) and Rob Baughman of Penn (4.0 GPA, #1 in Penn senior class). Dames gives a talk on behalf of all the Scholar Athlete Award finalists: "The self-discipline, teamwork, and respect you learn by participating in sports will help you be more successful in the classroom as well as in the work world. Each successful student has an internal drive which motivates them to do their best, but they also have an external motivator. On the football field the motivator is probably a coach. Anyone who has ever played football surely has had the pleasant experience of having your nice, calm, nurturing coach quietly explain to you, in that way that only a coach can, that the missed block, dropped pass, or missed tackle may have been your fault and that you might consider trying to correct those tiny little mistakes. This friendly reminder usually occurs just after he throws his headset and just before he kicks the water-boy." Laughter fills the room. Ben goes on to thank, on behalf of the Scholar Athletes, the parents, friends, teachers, coaches, and all those who provided support to them. "Finally, I would like to leave you with this quote that might describe the attitudes of the 10 finalists for the Student Athlete Award, and the attitude that is required to be a success: 'Far better it is to dare mighty things, to win glorious triumphs even though checkered by failure, than to rank with those poor spirits who neither enjoy much nor suffer much, because they live in the gray twilight that knows not victory nor defeat.'"

The Krause Chapter of the College Football Hall of Fame always welcomes new members. You can join. Heck. If they let Tom Dennin and John Fineran in, they'll let anybody in! Seriously, it costs $40 to join and the experiences involved and the friendships gained are worth 40 times that! Call 219-282-4828 and become a part of the legend of Moose Krause. Moose was always so nice to me. I remember one cold, rainy night in 1989 I had invited him to come to the WSBT radio studio in the evening to do a live interview about the Burger King Holiday Basketball Tournament he helped endorse. The weather became sloppy and I tried to call him at home to tell him not to bother battling the elements. He was getting up in years. Lo and behold, in walked Moose with a big trench coat and umbrella. He sat down and spent 20 minutes with me on the old Burger King Thursday night radio show. Gerry Krause said it best: "They talk about the Gipper, Rockne, and the Four Horsemen, but the true legend of Notre Dame was Moose Krause."

Taking Care of Wild Animals and Reflections of a Baseball Coaching Great

Today I get to see a deer walk upstairs in someone's rural Goshen house. I'm at the 70-acre refuge of Nancy Cobb and her family to tape a "Making a Difference" feature. Nancy makes a difference in the lives of injured and orphaned wild animals. She runs the Heartland Wildlife Rehabilitation Center and this time of the year she's so busy she hardly ever gets to sleep. That's because Nancy, and some of her volunteer helpers, are constantly nursing baby squirrels, raccoons, opossums, and other wild animals that have been brought to her home. Most of the animals are there because of humans. As she feeds baby squirrels with a bottle, she tells me a family cut down its evergreen tree without thinking a nest might be at the top. The mother squirrel barked frantically at the family, but to no avail. After gently putting the squirrels back in their box, Nancy picks up two baby raccoons that were kicked out of someone's chimney. They lost their mother in the process and cry constantly for her. All of these animals, and many more, ended up with Nancy. She'll nurture them and eventually place many of them on their refuge. There are various food sights on the land that help the animals until they get into the flow of coming up with their own chow out in the woods.

Nancy started caring for wild animals when she was very young. She and her sister would tell their parents about orphaned wild animals they found. Her love of wildlife led her to become a licensed wildlife rehabilitator. "My 20 years of experience as a rehabber have shown me a pattern in which 90% of my cases are 'man caused,'" Nancy says. "They are hit by cars, caught in leg hold traps, and entangled in our fences, string, or fishing line. We bail young fawns with hay unintentionally each year and til up bunny nests in our gardens and slaughter them while cutting the grass because we didn't 'walk' the area first. Raccoons, squirrels, and birds are orphaned because man chose "spring time" to cut down that old, hollow tree."

Nancy says that we all should avoid cutting down hollow trees during the springtime because they are often used for nests and dens. If you're driving and see a opossum that's been hit by a car, check to see if there's any babies in the pouch that are still alive. And just because you see baby rabbits alone doesn't mean they're orphaned. Nancy says the mother usually stays away from the nest because they are easier for predators to see. Before disturbing a nest, make sure they are orphaned.

Nancy takes me and WSBT's dashing French photographer Laurent on a tour of their refuge. "JOY!!" she cries out. "JOY!!" Out of the woods comes a bounding female deer. Joy was dragged out of the woods by a rottweiler when she was a fawn. Nancy was given the deer, rehabilitated it, and released her into the nearby woods. Joy follows us as we walk along streams to a cozy cabin tucked away next to the woods. For a donation that's used to buy nursing formula, folks can stay in the two-bed cabin overnight. It's an enchanting spot because wildlife flock around it in the evening. You have to "rough" it a little. There's an outhouse next to it along with a water pump. Inside are kerosene lamps with two single beds. I guarantee you it would be a unique experience that you don't find many places at all!

As we work our way back to the main house Nancy shows us a drake mallard that was hit by a car in Goshen. Nancy is slowly working it back to health. Then Nancy shows us Squirt, the orphaned SKUNK she raised. Squirt is fully capable of squirting! "We have a trusting relationship," Nancy tells me as I start backing up. As we get by the front porch, Joy the deer strides right into the house and up the stairs! "Don't go in the bedrooms," Nancy tells Joy from the bottom of the stairs. "Joy can't come down the stairs so I'll have to carry her down," Nancy tells us as we pack up our gear for the drive back to WSBT.

Unfortunately, there is no funding for wildlife rehabilitation. That puts Nancy and the animals in a bind. For at least three months in the springtime her formula needs total about $150 a week, let along unforeseen veterinary bills. Each year the numbers of cases increase causing her savings account to diminish. She and her husband can't do it alone. If you can help out financially give the Heartland Wildlife Rehabilitation Center a call at (219) 534-9686. Your family or organization can also visit the refuge. My visit ranks among the most rewarding and interesting things I've covered since I started doing the "Making a Difference" features!

Upon getting back to WSBT I just about fall over backwards as I'm told Ken Schreiber is retiring. The legendary LaPorte baseball coach is stepping down in his 39th season. A bleeding ulcer is part of the reason, but Schreiber has always maintained that when all the factors told him it was time to step down, he'd do it no matter if it were in the middle of a season or not. Ken Schreiber won 1,010 baseball games, seven State Championships, 25 Conference Championships, and on and on. I got to know him over the years as he often sat the same table I did at Notre Dame Quarterback Club luncheons. His good buddy Tim Lane of "sunny South Bend" was nice enough to invite us to sit at his table many times. I remember one time major league manager Jim "Mr. Vibrant" Leyland came to a luncheon with Dick "Mr. Reserved" Vitale, and Schreiber went over to say hello to Leyland. My buddy Steve Garner was visiting from St. Louis and snapped a picture of the two with his camera.

Former Slicer shortstop Chip Jones does the radio play-by-play of LaPorte games for WCOE-FM. In a column for the *Town Crier*, Jones shared his insight as to why Schreiber was so successful. Jones wrote about the incredible work ethic of Schreiber, his organization, and attention to detail ("he had his strategies figured out in advance for every situation"), and his teaching ability. Then Jones explained why Schreiber was the best at coaching baseball. "Though Schreiber coached many great players, he did not trot the most gifted and talented nine players onto the field 1,010 times. So why was he so successful? He was better than anyone else at teaching his students/players how to *compete*. It is human nature to accept less than your best, to find a comfort level and be satisfied. He would not allow it. It is easy to make excuses, 'I lost the ball in the sun,' or 'The umpire made a bad call.' Not acceptable in Schreib's world. He ruffled more than a few feathers pushing his students to do more than they thought they could or wanted to do. The bottom line is he got it done. His students learned, excelled and did it the right way. That is successful teaching."

LaPorte boys basketball coach Joe Otis has taught next door to Schreiber in the Social Studies Department since Otis got to Orange and Black country in 1980. Otis penned these thoughts on Schreiber for this book: "Ken Schreiber has brought a devotion to his craft unequaled by any coach in America. He has won all those games and titles. His field, Schrieber Field, the field that he built and continued to maintain all these years, has won numerous awards and twice been named National High School Diamond of the Year. He helped start the Indiana High School Baseball Tournament and the Indiana Baseball Coaches Association. He has served on the National Rules Committee and in countless other committees and organizations. After being around him all these years I have learned that his great talent is his passion for all things baseball. He loves the game, the equipment, the field, the history, the strategy, the stats, the sportswriters, his coaches, his players, the fans, and, most of all, the smell of victory. Ken Schreiber's genius as a coach was as simple as the game itself. He taught everyone around him to love the game as much as he did. Once they learned this lesson, taking their game to a higher level came naturally and the hard work, dedication, commitment, and sacrifice made the smell of victory so much sweeter." Otis concluded his thoughts on Schreiber with this quote from the great Jackie Robinson: "A life is not important except in the impact it has on other lives."

It's hard to picture LaPorte without Schreiber, but coaching legends eventually have to retire. Schreiber handles his departure news conference on this day with grace and class. Those around him get all torn up with emotion. When Matt Burridge gets back from the news conference, he says he had never seen so many people weeping off to the side. The Orange and Black have a bright future. Their tradition-rich past is secure because of Ken Schreiber.

This evening is highlighted by Bob Hammel's visit to South Bend. The veteran sportswriter and author is reading at the first H.O.P.E.

Literary Festival at St. Joseph's High School (alma mater of Phil Patnaude). St. Joe English teacher Diane Fox is the "adult" part of H.O.P.E. (Helping Other People Endure). These students serve at Hope Rescue Mission as well as work on food drives and food banks. They work year round on projects that help those in need. Hammel and other authors have come in this week to read and meet with the public. Money raised will go to H.O.P.E.

Hammel's a "delightful chap" who we often interview to get his insight on IU basketball. Tonight, he tells us the Hoosiers will probably be a guard-oriented team in 1999 that might press more than in the past. My friend Tim Lane used to bring me "Hammel IU articles" from the Bloomington paper over the years. He can flat out write.

The 1-800 Number
Silver Hawks' Mystery

I'm at Kennedy School on Olive Street in South Bend today. They've invited me to come out and read to Miss Colleen Waldron's fourth grade class and answer questions from the students. Laura McGann initially asked me to visit their school. Laura's in charge of parent involvement in Title One. Laura's a top flight runner who is married to Tim McGann. From what I understand, Tim is a near perfect husband who is never grumpy. He is sort of lumpy.

Sixth grade student Cordell Martin greets me in the lobby and shows me where I'm going to read. As we head to the stairs Aaron Demeter and Justin Harroff hit me up for a donation. They're raffling off a quilt with the money raised going to the Charles Martin Youth Center. Charles Martin was (and will always remain) a South Bend hero so I gladly buy some tickets. It's "Turn Off the TV Week" (except, of course, for programming on WSBT) at Kennedy. The students are focusing on the many wonderful things there are to read at their school and everywhere they go. After reading to them I take their questions, which is always an unpredictable and fun experience.

"HOW MUCH MONEY DO YOU MAKE?"

"HAVE YOU MET MICHAEL JORDAN?" ("Yes. I've interviewed him two or three times, but I seriously doubt he remembers me.")

"HOW TALL ARE YOU?" (6' 5" or 6' 6")

"WILL YOU PUT US ON TV?"

"DO YOU KNOW PEYTON MANNING?"

There are many more serious questions too, but I always have to be on the balls of my feet to answer questions from fourth graders. I have to be in A STATE OF ALERTNESS! I really am impressed with my visit to Kennedy, home of the Road Runners. The students are very polite and respectful to me. As some of the questions revealed, they also show me their fun personalities. Vermario Napper escorts me to the door when it's time to leave.

Visits like this always put me in good spirits as I get to work. I love being around teachers and administrators and seeing the daily impact they have on the lives of young students.

The "unexpected development of the day" revolves around a feature that Mike Stack does for the 10 PM newcast. It's on the close relationship Silver Hawks infielder Jared Martin has with his dad. Jared's father lives in Florida. To keep up with his son's progress in minor league baseball, he has called WSBT-AM 960 radio the past two years. He's had the guy on the programming board connect his phone line so he could listen to the whole Silver Hawks game on radio. Stack's story is touching as Jared talks about how much his dad's support means to him. Mike and I were under the impression that Dad Martin was footing the long distance phone bill. Actually, he was calling the 1-800 number of the radio station because they thought that didn't cost anyone anything. Woops. WSBT Radio general manager Sally Brown happened to see the story air on the TV news and had radio news director Bob "Muscles" Montgomery check into the deal. As it turns out, the 1-800 number was costing WSBT about 11 cents a minute. Seeing as how the Silver Hawks play about 140 games a year that are three hours each, it's easy to see why Bob's eyes popped out when he realized what happened. Dad Martin felt awful about it and volunteered to pay for the calls. WSBT said it was okay and an honest mistake on all parties involved. Little did Mike Stack and I know that a feature on a dad and his Silver Hawk son would lead to the "1-800 Investigation!"

APRIL
Wednesday
29

Career Day

I'm all over the place this week. Public appearances seem to get scheduled in droves. There will be one week where I don't go anywhere. Then there will be another week when I'm invited to speak or appear all over creation.

This morning I'm at Twin Branch School Career Day. Jeanie Butterfield and Claudia Toelke are the co-chairpersons of their first Career Day and are bubbling with enthusiasm as I get to the Mishawaka school. They've done a great job coordinating the day. Jeannie's mother, Mildred Johnston, has a place in Indiana sports history. Mildred was one of the first, if not *the* first women to coach varsity *boys*' teams, including track, basketball, and baseball. Mildred took over the programs in 1945, after Liberty High School's coach went into the service in World War II. Mildred, who had been a basketball star at IU, was in charge of the boys teams for two years. Terry Johnston, her son, was the team's mascot. He would go on to be a judge. Among her players in basketball was Fred "Miss it" Bachman.

At Twin Branch, there are all sorts of firemen, authors, military officers, policemen, and sportscasters like me on hand. Having appeared at many Career Days over the years in Michiana, I've learned that the first thing to do is find the teachers' break room. That's where the donuts always are sitting. I always plow through two to three before guiding students towards their professional future.

Twin Branch School is first-rate. It's been a 4-Star school four times. It has a well-known Gifted and Talented program. Twin Branch has received the highest ISTEP scores in Mishawaka several times. The school is sharper than a tack.

During the morning, I spend some time with Principal Steve Van Bruaene. Steve loves to play golf like Luke Choate. He also is a dynamic principal who is "pioneering" the CLASS program. It's 16 life skills and five lifelong guidelines that he put together when some parents at his previous school, LaSalle Elementary, revealed they felt the students were not learning enough citizenship in schools. Steve believes the young students learn best when they can connect it to something. He says Corporate America is looking for more than academic ability. That's where CLASS comes in. Here are the 16 life skills:

PERSEVERANCE: To continue in spite of difficulties.

PATIENCE: To wait calmly for someone or something.

COOPERATION: To work together toward a common goal or purpose.

ORGANIZATION: To plan, arrange and implement in an orderly way.

FLEXIBILITY: The ability to alter plans when necessary.

PROBLEM SOLVING: To seek solutions in difficult situations.

CURIOSITY: A desire to learn or know about a full range of things.

RESPONSIBILITY: To be accountable for your actions.

COURAGE: The quality of mind that enables one to face danger or hardship with confidence.

INTEGRITY: To act according to what's right and wrong.

COMMON SENSE: To think it through.

SENSE OF HUMOR: To laugh and be playful without hurting others.

EFFORT: To try your hardest.

FRIENDSHIP: To make and keep a friend through mutual trust and caring.

COURAGE: The quality of mind that enables one to face danger or hardship with confidence.

PRIDE: Satisfaction from doing your personal best.

This CLASS program is impressive and I can see where it would be so important in the educational development of the youngsters. Steve's previous school, LaSalle Elementary, is a model sight for CLASS. If you want to learn more about CLASS, contact Steve at Twin Branch School in Mishawaka. He also will provide analysis of your golf swing.

Career Day goes great, except for the firetruck that's parked right in front of my car with a bunch of enthralled youngsters around it. I don't want to ask them to move it for me since the kids are having such a good time, so I back up and drive across the school lawn to the road. Of course, others then stare at me like I'm half baked in the head.

After taking care of the 5:00 and 6:00 sportscasts back at the station, I put on the proud, bright red uniform of the WSBT All-Stars! Our charity basketball team is playing in Buchanan, Michigan, tonight to raise money for the Buchanan Police Explorers. Bethel College star Rico Swanson comes to WSBT and rides with me up to the gym. I tell Rico that since meteorologist Bob Werner and reporter Ed Ernstes cannot play with us that we have a good chance to actually win. They both have prior commitments. Sometimes I consider telling them our games are in Angola or Grissom Air Force Base to get the athletically-challenged Bob and Ed as far away from the real game location as possible.

T.J. Shidecker is the sophomore who arranges this game. I have admired his determination all along to put together such a benefit. The folks in Buchanan greet us warmly as we arrive. It's a tight-knit community that always comes together for causes like this. The Police Explorers program enables the high school students to train and help with the Berrien County Youth Fair, traffic control during city events, fingerprinting area youth, and being role models to area youth. Before the game, I stand at the door and encourage/bug/hassle folks to buy WSBT coffee mugs for $10 each. All that money goes to the Explorers.

Behind Rico, we go on to beat the local police and firefighters, 77-62. Of course, they're exhausted from having fought a big fire in Buchanan the night before, but we'll take the win. Being the big shot "General Manager" of the All-Stars, I get to rustle up all our sweaty uniforms and haul them back home. They usually sit in the back of my truck until the next game. Sometimes I wash them. Sometimes I don't.

An NFL Great Visits South Bend

As you've read in this book, I like to play jokes on folks. I've pulled a few pranks on Hedge Harridge, who handles public relations for the College Football Hall of Fame. Well, the night before the famous and eagerly awaited Lynn Swann is to speak before a big crowd in downtown South Bend, Hedge leaves me a frantic voice mail at WSBT.

"Charlie! Lynn Swann has the flu. We have to have a speaker for the Gridiron Legends Luncheon. PLEASE fill in for us tomorrow! Call me ASAP!!"

My heart skips a beat as I hear the message. About 300 folks have paid $15 to hear Lynn Swann, a man who played on four Steelers Super Bowl champs and a national championship team at Southern California. So many tickets have been sold that the luncheon has been moved from the Press Box of the Hall of Fame across the street to the Century Center. I doubt very seriously those that bought tickets are going to be thrilled to see ol' Charlie walk up to the podium and rattle on about college football. I can just picture Hall Executive Director Bernie Kish introducing me. "Charlie never played College Football, but he's our speaker in a pinch. Here's Charlie." A smattering of applause would follow. Actually, Bernie would spruce up my intro much better than that.

After hearing the message I go find the fountain of experience and wisdom, veteran news anchor Mike Collins. "What should I do, Mike? They're in a bad situation, but those people that paid for tickets are expecting Lynn Swann—not the local sportscaster who never played college ball." Mike tells me to go by my instincts. He reminds me of Yoda in Star Wars. I stew over this for 15 minutes before calling Hedge back.

"Hedge. I really think you should get someone from Notre Dame. Or how about Joe Yonto. Tom Pagna. I don't feel good about this. I'll do it, but...."

"Charlie," Hedge says. "FOOLED YA! Lynn Swann is fine. He'll be there."

AARRRGH! This time I'M the victim of a joke! I hold the phone away from my ear as Hedge cackles hysterically for 45 seconds. Actually, I have a sense of relief because I would have had to go into immediate "Speech Preparation."

On this Thursday morning, a healthy and vibrant Lynn Swann does arrive in South Bend. He tours the College Football Hall of Fame and raves about its appeal to all ages. "One will get a true sense of what it's like to be on a team," Swann says. The ABC sportscaster obliges the autograph requests he gets before the luncheon at Century Center begins. A lot of local Steelers fans are on hand with memorabilia. Swann was the NFL Man of the Year for his community service during his pro football days. It's a shame that he hasn't been elected to the Pro Football Hall of Fame.

The plum prize of his trip is getting to sit at a table of Norwest Bank employees during the lunch. There's not much in life that tops that. After being introduced, Swann gives a memorable and fun talk that reflects his intelligence and character. He shares how he came to be. Lynn's mom and dad had two boys, which set up this "dialogue between the two parents."

DAD SWANN: "Two kids. No more!"

MOM SWANN: "One more. Let's try for a girl!"

DAD SWANN: "No. I'm working hard at my job! Two is enough."

MOM SWANN: "I say we try for another!"

Dad Swann had a couple of scotches and Mom won!

Swann tells the audience that while growing up he thought about becoming a dancer, actor, or lawyer. "I guess that's redundant," Swann says to laughs. "Dancer. Actor. Lawyer."

With football players from Washington High and Penn at the luncheon, Swann shares valuable advice. "When I speak to young people, I try to get across that if you have a choice about your future, do something that you care about and want to do in life. You then take ownership for your decision because YOU made the decision. It's something you believe in, not something your parents or someone else wants you to do or feels you should do." Swann, who has a degree in Public Relations and a minor in Psychology, stressed another point to high school students. Their future employers will obviously look at the academic success, but much more as well. "Who you are and what you're able to do is not your grade point average. Who you are is what you make of yourself. If you don't give the effort in class that you give to fooling around with friends, then you are selling yourself short. Everything takes time. People in the job market want to see that you set a goal and reached the goal. Most of us don't use the particular degree we get in college, but getting a college degree shows we can set a goal and reach it over a period of years."

All of this certainly hits home with me, and hopefully many high school students that read this book. As I remember, I made a 15 or 16 on the ACT, which is blah. I had a mediocre GPA in High School. I regret not making better grades and applying myself more academically, but I never felt I was my GPA. I battled through college but reached my goal of getting a degree. In my case it was in Education. Like Swann said, I'm one of the folks who hasn't used my exact degree, but I would not have become a sportscaster without finishing college. Reaching the finish line of college gave me great confidence as well as all sorts of knowledge.

As Lynn Swann said, who you are is *what you make of yourself.* Former Notre Dame great and Chicago Bear Chris Zorich is a great example. His grades were not all that hot, but he made himself into a community servant through his football success. He's going to Law School to that he can help pass laws that benefit inner-city youngsters. Zorich has touched more lives than many reclusive 3.9 GPA-types who bury themselves in a computer.

After the luncheon, I rush back to WSBT to meet photographer Laurent. We drive to Dickinson Middle School in South Bend to tape an upcoming "Making a Difference" feature. I recently got a nice letter urging me to do a feature on Howard Edwards, a 1982 LaSalle High grad.

Howard was a heckuva basketball player who was part of some great games between LaSalle and Scott Skiles' Plymouth Pilgrims. Howard went on to get his college degree at IUSB in Special Education. He would tack on two master's degrees in Education. Along the way he also graduated from the Indiana Law Enforcement Academy. These days Howard holds two jobs. He teaches at Dickinson Middle School (as well as being the athletic director). He also is a police officer with the South Bend Police Department. Howard is also a loving husband and father of three! "This man is a local home town hero," the letter proclaims, and I agree.

Howard is part of the South Bend Police Department's Bike Patrol. He is among the first to be on the midnight patrol downtown. Many days he puts in a full day at Dickinson, goes home to his family, and then patrols downtown from 11 PM to 7 AM. He rides by WSBT often where he can keep an eye on that troublemaker Jack Reichert. Being a police officer helps the impact he makes on the youth of Dickinson Middle School. "Most kids there know I'm a police officer," Howard says. "I do talk to them of the consequences of their actions here at school. They listen to me a little more where probably if I didn't have the title of police officer I wouldn't make as much difference." Howard tells me he is a Christian who credits his mother and grandmother for making sure he was in church regularly as a youngster. By being a Special Education teacher he helps the youngsters that need a little more time to grasp the subjects. "Not all students can learn at a fast rate," Howard says. Howard's a big fan of Notre Dame and the Dallas Cowboys. When I tell him I heard Lynn Swann earlier in the day, he flinches, "Swann hurt my Irish in College and he got my Cowboys in the Super Bowl!"

MAY
Wednesday
6

Talking Leadership in Warsaw

Ring! Bob Follett, athletic director at Dowagiac High School, calls me at WSBT. He's in a pinch. "Charlie, our All-Sports Banquet is coming up at the end of this month. We had (baseball great) Carlton Fisk lined up as our speaker, but he's had to back out. Can you be the speaker?"

Not for a second am I "irritated" to be the second choice. The All-Sports banquet at Dowagiac has a great tradition for dynamic speakers. Over the years, Ara Parseghian, Heisman winner Johnny Lujack, Duffy Daugherty, Jud Heathcote, Marv Wood, Ray Meyer, and Gale Sayers have been among their speakers. They swing for the fence when trying to line up the big names. This year it just so happened that Fisk had to back out.

"What day is it on, Bob?"

He tells me Thursday, May 28th. I glance at my calendar with all my chicken scratch writing on it. That particular day looks clear. The Acordia Special Olympics golf outing at Juday Creek is the day before, but the 28th will work.

"Count me in, Bob."

He tells me about 400 will be in attendance. Hopefully, they'll know beforehand that I'm the speaker and not Carlton Fisk. I can just picture some fella at a front table throwing rolls at me and bonking me in the head because he was looking forward to Fisk telling about his Game 6 homer against the Reds where he waved the ball fair.

With Mike handling the sportscasts, I leave WSBT and drive down to Warsaw. I pull up to the Center Lake Pavilion to speak at the fifth Kosciusko Youth Leadership Academy banquet. Twenty-five students from the junior classes at the county schools Warsaw, Tippecanoe Valley, Wawasee, Whitko and Triton have been a part of the year-long program designed, in part, to develop leadership skills. It's a dynamic program that should be used by more schools. The students heard talks throughout the year from area leaders. The students also designed and implemented programs that did good things for their community.

Before my talk, Miss Kosciusko Erin Cassidente performs two songs. In between, she tells everyone something she heard in church recently. "The preacher told us, 'Live your life in a way where I don't have to lie at your funeral.'" That got a good laugh. Actually, it's a pretty effective way of putting it. Think about it.

During my talk, one of the points I try to get across is that as a leader (sports director) I try to get reporters to get more out of a story than what they originally *think they're capable of*. As an example, I tell them of the time Warsaw's Kevin Ault was named the prestigious Mr. Basketball. After getting word at the station, Matt Burridge loaded up his camera and got ready to go down and do a story on Kevin. He intended to do an interview at Kevin's house and bring it back and put together a solid but basic story. I encouraged Matt to think of a way to make the story even better. He started brainstorming. "Why don't you ask Kevin where he shot baskets so much as a kid," I suggested. "Take him there and have him reflect at the place where he put in so many hours."

Matt liked that a lot. When he got down there, he asked Kevin where that place was. Kevin went to his closet and got out an old leather ball that's cover was almost totally worn off. He and Matt walked to a nearby elementary school and Matt shot video of Kevin shooting at the hoop where he had taken thousands of shots as a kid growing up dreaming of being Mr. Basketball.

MAY
Monday
11

Turning Their Lives Around

"My goal was to spend my life in jail."

That's what a young man tells me today during an interview for Turnaround Achievement series. Newsroom secretary/producer Jennifer Addington has arranged the interview. It's the second of a three-part series I'm doing in News this month leading into the second annual South Bend Turnaround Achievement Awards program on May 20th. Ray Hess and the folks at Chippewa Bowl have teamed up with Jon Backstrom and everyone at Beacon Bowl to create this inspirational awards program. "We believe businesses should become involved with their local schools and assist educators in meeting America 2000 and other state and country education goals," says Mark Voight, owner of the Community Bowling Centers chain. "We also believe the Turnaround Achievement Awards program helps educators address the dropout problem facing all our schools." TCI of Michiana and WSBT have also been a part in it since its inception in 1997. WSBT President and General Manager Jim Freeman was a driving force on our part. Jim cares deeply for the community and how WSBT can give back.

We arrive at Washington High School at 1 PM to interview a young man who at one point wanted to live his life in prison so he could get big muscles. We pop into the office to say hello to secretary Pat Czarnecki, who has been there 43 years (a proud Panther alum, also!). Senior Sarah Wood is in the office also. A delightful young lady, she tells me about how well her older brother Matt is doing with the Ball State baseball team. Matt was the winner of the prestigious Burger King, WSBT High School Athlete of the Year in 1996. Assistant Principal Michael Sacchini greets us along with Leonora Battani, the Bilingual Education Specialist at WHS. As we walk down the hall, Leonara gives me grief for not showing more Riley highlights. Her children go there. I tell her that we show the Wildcats as much as the Panthers, Lions, Colonials, Eagles, and so on, but she still gives me a hard time. We stop near the library and Leonora goes to get Juan Carlos Orona from class. While I wait, I talk with Assistant Principal Sacchini, who is a true hometown hero. His dedication to helping youngsters of all races is to be admired. When you talk about those who make a difference in the lives of young people who have gotten off the tracks, he is at the top of the list. Michael has dealt with a lot of interesting and challenging young folks, but based on what he tells me in the hallway, Juan Carlos has to be the "humdinger" of them all. He is a sophomore that was "due processed" (expelled for a year, basically) out of Washington last year because of behavioral problems.

Juan Carlos walks up and shakes my hand. He's a handsome, fit young man with a nice smile and a clean haircut. He settles into a chair and photographer Laurent hooks a microphone to his collar.

"I always wanted to be a big gang member and run my own gang," he tells me. We're sitting in an aisle in the library. Rows of books surround us. "I wanted to go to prison. I was always doing whatever was bad. I got locked up one time and I was like, 'I like this. I could be here for the rest of my life.' I wanted to have a big record where people would say, 'man, this is a troublemaker!' If somebody said 'let's go do this' and it was bad, I'd say, 'let's go!' We'd go rob a car, or just go get high. I didn't really care. I just wanted to do whatever was bad."

That's when Washington High School, after doing everything they could to swing him back, showed him the exit door. His loving family, in an effort to get him away from trouble, moved him to Florida where he started working in the fields as a vegetable picker. That kind of work sent him a quick message. "I found out I didn't want that kind of job," he says. I can picture him stooping over in the brutal humidity with insects all around. "I was working real hard for a few dollars. I was like, 'forget this, I'm going to school.'

Juan Carlos did go back and was doing okay, getting B's and C's. He went to night school. Still, there was a pattern of drinking and weed on Saturday nights that often left him still high when his family took him to church on Sundays. "One of my pastors said they wanted to send me to a camp at their expense. I went down there and was looking for trouble. A kid had a joint and I said, 'let's go fire it up.' So we went into the woods and lit it up. I came back to the place where we all ate and got real sick. I felt like I was about to die, and then I seen somebody who was, like, real into God and I went to him to see if he would pray for me and he prayed for me. Ever since that day I gave up smoking weed and that was the last step I needed to take."

Juan Carlos's grades started getting better in school. "I always liked sports," he says. "That was one of the reasons I wanted to go to prison. The guys in there, man, they're big! I was like, 'I want to be like that.' But instead of prison and lifting weights, I chose sports and it helped me keep out of trouble and learn to respect others, especially wrestling. I like wrestling. We have practice for two or two-and-a-half hours after school (with highly respected coach Carl Evans). When I get home, I'm too tired to get into trouble."

Juan Carlos kept striving in the classroom and made the Honor Roll at Washington for the fall semester of 1997. "My goal is to get a good paying job. I'll do whatever it takes. I like learning. I like learning new skills. Gangs is not anywhere to go. If kids want money, education is where the money is. I figure it like this: If you receive A's and B's, that's a good paying job. C's are an average paying job. D's and F's, that's a job nobody wants."

Afterwards, Leonora tells me the key to his turnaround was the support from his family and the support structure at school. The system is there in the school to help, but a youngster has to believe in himself to make it happen. Juan Carlos believed in himself, and that opened the door for everyone to help him.

Juan Carlos and I talk a little bit before I have to get back to the station and prepare the evening sportscasts. We then shake hands as I head to the WSBT News car. "I wouldn't want to go back to gangs," he says. "If I could change my life all over again. . . .I would have stuck to school. That way I'd have graduated by now!"

Mike Stack's All-Time Favorite Chicago Cubs

Cubs fans throughout the building at WSBT are all wound up about Kerry Wood today. The flame-throwing pitcher mowed down 13 Diamondbacks Monday night. Surely, glory days are ahead for the Cubbies now that they have him.

As described earlier in this book, Mike Stack has been a Cubs fan since he was six. Now 30 years old, his team of all-time "Favorite Cubs" reflects his generation (no Cubs from way back on his team—I mean how can you not have Ernie Banks on this kind of team!?). Here now is Stack's Favorite Cubbies along with selected comments from Stack:

RHP—RICK SUTCLIFFE: Without him, no 1984 or 1989 division titles. He was a true leader. And whenever there was a fight, kind of like when Eric Show drilled Andre Dawson in the face, Sutcliffe was always the first one out of the dugout ready to make somebody pay.

LHP—STEVE TROUT: Also, without him, no 1984 titles. He was a little flaky, but he had some wicked pitches. You've got to root for a guy who injures himself falling off an exercise bike.

RELIEF PITCHER—BRUCE SUTTER: Until hitters learned to lay off the split-finger fastball, he was untouchable. Whenever he came on in the eighth or ninth, even though Jack Brickhouse sounded worried, I knew the game was in the bag. "Everybody exhale now!"

LEFT FIELD—GARY MATTHEWS: Once again, no Sarge, no '84 titles. Not the most graceful outfielder, but with Bob Dernier to his left and the Bleacher Bums behind him, the Sarge could do no wrong.

CENTER FIELD—BOB DERNIER: This guy was a bullet in the outfield and on the bases. Part one of the Cubs' "Daily Double," Dernier had a career year in '84.

RIGHT FIELD—ANDRE DAWSON: Anyone with his ability who will sign for only $500,000 just so he could play for my Cubs is an all-time favorite. Andre brought leadership and respect back to the North Side. He could hit, run, field, and had an arm like a Howitzer. I'm definitely part of "Andre's Army!"

THIRD BASE—RYNE SANDBERG: As a rookie, the hot corner belonged to Ryno. He made playing third look so effortless. In a position at Wrigley held by the likes of Ron Cey, Keith Moreland, and Ken Reitz, ugh, there's no doubt that Ryne has a lock on third.

SHORTSTOP—SHAWON DUNSTON: Not the most disciplined, but certainly the most exciting Cub I've watched. I loved watching him stretch a single into a double capped off by the belly flop at second. To see him go from first to third on a SAC bunt was also a thrill. And, oh, what an arm!!

SECOND BASE—RYNO: Need I say more?

FIRST BASE—MARK GRACE: He's a throwback to the days of when baseball players were baseball players. Always hustling, always looking to do the right things with the bat depending on the situation. Grace will go down as one of the all-time great Cubs. Too bad he wasn't around at first for Game 5 of the '84 NLCS. Leon Durham might still be playing!

CATCHER—JODY DAVIS: Joe-deee! Joe-deee! Davis, like many on the team, had a career year in '84. He caught something like 145 games that year and I think that may have shortened his career. In following years, Jody swung a very tired bat. But because of his service in 1984, Jody's the man behind the plate.

MANAGER—JIM FREY: He was a crafty guy full of fire. Plus, he brought me my first championship as a Cub fan. But he started to think a little too much in the '84 NLCS. Should have gone with Sutcliffe in Game 4. We'd still be talking about that World Series sweep over the Tigers! (Spoken like a true Cub fan!)

FAVORITE ALL-TIME CUB—BILL BUCKNER. Please don't laugh. Buckner gave the Cubs all he had on two bum wheels. He hustled, he got dirty. Bill Buckner was a gamer! I know what he'll forever be remember for, so I won't even bring it up, but when I was growing up watching the Cubs, before '84 he was all they had. I would have kept him and traded Durham and a player to be named later for Eckersley. Unfortunately, the Cubs were always the butt of those joke trades! Hang baseball's Purple Heart on Bill Buckner—he gave the game all he could (McNamara should have taken him out for defensive purposes, anyway!).

Mike has formed the Cubs Fan Club of South Bend-Mishawaka. If you'd like to join, contact Mike at (219) 273-8489.

On this Tuesday evening, the WSBT All-Star Basketball team wobbles its way down to LaVille Elementary School to battle the faculty and staff. The money raised is to be split between the Elementary Library Fund and the Junior Scout Troop that organized the game. Mrs. Whitaker's troop 411 put the game together to help fund their June trip to a dude ranch (HEY! I never got to go to a dude ranch when I was in Elementary School!!).

The Big Boss Man, Superintendent Robert Huffman, and the rest of the LaVille team outnumber us 23 to 7. Depth, again, will be a problem for us. We battle valiantly and force the game into overtime. Then, much to our horror, all of the 23 LaVille players take the court. We have just five. The referee ignores this blatant substitution violation and we go on to lose, 54-52, as LaVille Elementary School assistant principal Alan Metcalfe scores the winning bucket. He does so as part of a 13-on-3 fast break.

The game attracts a near capacity crowd, which tells you the kind of support the community gives to its school and kids. LaVille principal John Farthing tells us that the school makes $1,300 off the game—the largest fundraiser of this kind in the history of the school. It just goes to show you that if Norm Stangland is running around in shorts and a tank top, the people will come out. I was really impressed with the job Mrs. Burden and Miss Carll did with their cheerleaders, posters, and banners. One of the posters has pictures of both teams. It declares that the players with little heads are LaVille staff. The ones with big heads are WSBT All-Stars.

The Impact of ROTC

"I didn't care about anything."

I am listening to a high school student talk about how he used to be before making a remarkable turnaround in his life. Because of his admirable 180-degree swing, he is going to be one of those honored at the Century Center in South Bend. His name is Paul Batton. Paul is a senior at Riley High School. Because of ROTC, he is going to graduate and make a difference in society. Quite a turnaround from when he was a ninth grader at Riley.

"When I first came in the ROTC program, I tried to sleep in class," he reflects while decked out in his crisp, eye-catching uniform. "I really didn't care. I was getting D's and F's in school. Now, I get B's and C's with a few A's. I'm starting to respect my parents more. I'm a better citizen and I'm going out and helping with the community."

Paul's posture would make a chiropractic proud. He looks WSBT producer Jennifer Addington directly in the eye while answering her questions. Jennifer is one of the brightest and most versatile people we have in the newsroom. She's handling the interview for this particular "Making a Difference" feature.

Sgt. Roy Mullins nominated Paul for a Turnaround Achievement award. "Paul has made the biggest turnaround of all the four-year students that I've had in ROTC," says Sergeant Mullins. "Paul used to sleep all the time in all his classes. He didn't show much self esteem or pride at all. He's had a tough home life this past year with his parents separating and now divorcing." What ROTC did for Paul was help him grow up. It helped him handle the adversity in his life. "This program does help kids that are not really good at school," Paul says, attributing his turnaround completely to being in ROTC. "It brings you up. It's given me the push to graduate. I used to always have an attitude with my parents. I never respected them. We always fought. Now, we pretty much see eye to eye. I respect my brother and sister too. We used to argue and fight every day."

Behind Paul, on the wall in the classroom at Riley, is a ROTC sign that lists the goal of everyone in the program:
- 100% attendance at Drill, PT, and class
- Unit G.P.A. of 2.5 or higher
- Academic improvement in all subjects
- Become a better person and citizen

"One of the things Sarge told me," adds Paul, "is that there's a lot of room for losers, but there's more room for winners. When he said a winner, I said, 'Well, I'd love to be a winner. I'd actually like to graduate and accomplish something for myself,' because I really hadn't done much for myself because I just didn't care."

During his four years in ROTC, Paul worked his way into leadership positions. As a cadet captain, he was given many responsibilities. He followed them all through. "We're a Military Science program," Sergeant Mullins explains, "but we're not sitting here going 'you're going to go in the military.' We don't push that. Some kids may want to do that, and that's their choice, but I think we're trying to get their education first. Get them prepared for graduation, and then college or the workforce."

If you have kids that could benefit from the many positives of ROTC, contact your local high school for more information.

MAY
Sunday
18

Parading around Town While Jody Talks to My Sunday School Class

I'm the Grand Marshall of the Opening Day Parade of the Clay Junior Baseball and Softball Association today. Over the years I've had a chance to ride in many of these kinds of parades. They're always a blast. Fire engines accompany about a dozen pickup trucks full of Little Leaguers as they weave their way through neighborhood streets to the baseball diamonds.

Back in the early 1990s, I was in one of the parades that started *very* early one Saturday morning on the west side of South Bend. That was fine for most of the neighborhood folks. They were up early standing in the yards waving at us. But for those who had been out the night before partying into the wee hours, it was a different story. The firetruck sirens were blasting away LOUDLY and I was chipper Charlie. Inevitably, we came by the house of some guy who had been out until 3:30 AM the night before. His front door opened and out he wobbled. His hair looked like a squirrel's nest. He was wearing his boxers, cussing up a storm at us. My last glimpse of him as we rounded the corner was seeing him holding his head as he stumbled back in his house. I don't believe he quite caught the spirit of Little League Baseball at that particular time of the day. Perhaps later that afternoon.

On this Sunday, Sherrad, the kids, and I get to the 8:45 AM service at Evangel Heights. We hear a wonderful presentation from Mr. Bruce Yerry, director of the Hope Rescue Mission in South Bend, about how much the "Hope" means to those who are down and out. At about 9:45, I slip out of the service just before the closing hymn to look for Jody Martinez in the lobby. The former Bethel College basketball star, who is now the Women's Basketball Head Coach at Bethel, is going to speak to our youth in Sunday School. I greet Jody and thank him so much for coming to talk. I explain to him again that after introducing him I'm going to have to take off to make the parade. He understands, so down we go to the Sunday School room.

After telling the kids that Jody is Bethel's second leading all-time scorer (behind only Mark Galloway) and all his other accomplishments, I slip out the door and head to my car. As I drive north on Ironwood to Swanson Elementary School, this is part of what Jody shares with the middle school-aged kids in the class, as well as the many adults who have come down after hearing he was going to talk.

I've been around sports my whole life. My focus was bas-ketball. I dedicated my summer before my senior season at Marian High School to basketball. I didn't work a job. I didn't hang out with my buddies. I practiced basketball six to eight hours a day, seven days a week. I'm not talking about 5-on-5 full-court play-ground junkball. I mean ballhandling drills through the neighbor-hood and relentless wind sprints. I wanted to earn a college schol-arship. Your Christian life is like sports. You better be dedicated. Going to church one day a week ain't gonna cut it, because six days a week Satan has a crack at you. And six days to one, we're outnumbered.

My senior year, I was MVP of Marian. I made the All-Sec-tional team. I got scholarship offers from Valparaiso, Northeast Missouri State, Drake, a couple of small division-one schools, and Bethel College. I picked Bethel so I could be close to home and my younger brother, who I was very close to, could see me play. Bethel's a Christian school. I went there not being a Chris-tian. My junior year, I met my future wife, Sonya. She was a bas-ketball fanatic like me and a wonderful person. We got engaged my senior year.

After Bethel, I wanted to play professionally. I got an invitation to the NBA Rookie Camp in Chicago in 1990. Out of 100 players, just two were from the NAIA level and I was one of the them. Talk about a 'wakeup call,' I got one at that camp. I had been a center in college. There, they made me a wing player. I was okay at that position because of all the practice on ballhandling I did the summer before my senior season in high school. But I found out in a hurry that 6'8," 200 pounds is not going to cut it at the NBA level. It was too physical. Only one NBA team talked to me—the Los Angeles Clippers. They told me I needed to gain 40 pounds. I knew that wouldn't happen. I had been trying to gain weight my whole life.

I went to Mexico to play professionally. I had my Bible, but not once did I pick it up. The problem was, they treat you like royalty. When our team went on the road, most of the team went on a school bus. Myself and the other two American players rode with the president of the team in his Lincoln Continental. I made $3,000 a month. Cash. No taxes. The Mexican players? Maybe $100 a week. I was loving life, but I was missing something. I was a month away from my wedding. When I had become engaged, I made my priority to spend most of my time with her. Then, just before I was to fly back to get married, the team told me she couldn't come back with me. I was stunned. My agent flew down from Kansas City and they finally agreed that Sonya could come down, but couldn't travel on the road with us. Our team had stretches of two weeks at home and two weeks on the road. No way was I going on the road and leaving her alone in Chihuahua, Mexico.

I then made the decision to come home. No longer would I make all that money. I soon got an offer from the Columbus (OH) team in the Continental Basketball Association, but it was for just $1,000 a month. I had to make a decision. I gave up basketball. Foreign teams still went after me. At age 26, Luxembourg gave me one last offer of $50,000 a year. I turned it down. I had given up basketball in my life. Still, I was missing something. I worked a year at First Source Bank, but I found myself missing basketball. I went back to school so that I could become a coach.

Then, in January of 1992, I was in my wife's church. It was like the pastor was talking directly to me. Usually, I would be daydreaming, or checking things off in the bulletin as they happened so that I would know we were almost done with the service. That day, I got a weird sensation. In the Baptist Church, they give you a chance to come down front at the end of the service. I was sweating bullets. I grabbed my wife. "I don't know what's going on," I said. She's crying. We walked up front. "I think I need God in my life," I said to the pastor. "I have to, 'cause I don't know how else I got up here.' It took me a while to understand what salvation is all about. It's just a simple acceptance of Him. That Jesus died for us for our sins. Jesus was the greatest teacher ever on earth. He told stories, parables, that make you think. They apply to our lives. You know, one of the greatest things about being human is free will. God has given us the gift of free will. We know the difference between right and wrong. You can put on an act before your parents and teachers. But what happens when they turn around? There are two that you can never trick, lie to, or manipulate. One is you. You always know the truth. The second one is the man upstairs. The one who watches every single thing you do. But he is such a loving God he will forgive you because of the relationship you have developed with him. So I encourage you to develop your relationship with Jesus.

One thing I get all the time is, "Why are you smiling so much?" It's because I have God in me. My faith is so strong that no matter what comes my way I'm always smiling. But, as a basketball head coach, I soon found my priorities were out of line. I was head coach at LaVille High School, which is a wonderful place. But I had to make a change. In my life, God is first, family second, secondary family is third, and my job is fourth. I was spending 12 to 14 hours a day, six days a week, at LaVille as head basketball coach, assistant athletic director, and golf coach. When I spend that amount of time on priority #4, something is wrong with 1 and 2. They were getting cheated. As a new father, I never realized a baby would change my priorities so much. I lost all my passion for coaching high school basketball. Christmas break was coming up and I was spending maybe 10 hours a week with

*our two-month-old daughter. I went to our principal. I told him I
was not going to become someone who regrets not watching my
kids grow up. I didn't want to be remembered as a Bethel All-
American, or a head basketball coach. I wanted to be remembered for two things: a great Christian husband and a great Christian father. I resigned effective at the end of the school year.
After prayer, Bethel College asked me back to be their women's
head basketball coach. I said only if my wife could be my assistant coach. That way she goes everywhere I go. Our house was
right next to Bethel. No longer would I have long commutes. I
could walk home for lunch.*

*I really believe that ever since I became a dedicated Chris-
tian in 1992, that my blessings have been a thousand-fold. Right
now, I've challenged myself to read the whole Bible. I'm in Joshua
in the Old Testament. The thing is, I started in the New Testament. If you want to read the Bible, I suggest you start with the
New Testament. Read about Jesus. Then go to the Old Testament and read about the prophecies and everything.*

As the choir in an adjoining room practices for the 11:00 AM service, Jody concludes his talk and thanks everyone for inviting him to the
Sunday School.

Meanwhile, in north South Bend, I pull into Swanson Elementary
School where dozens of cars and pickups are already lined up for the
parade. I think I'm the only person in the history of church to be a Sunday School teacher who introduced his guest speaker to the class, then
went to the church bathroom to put on shorts and a T-shirt, and then
drove to be in a Little League baseball parade. With excited kids running around in their uniforms, Dennis Cooper greets me. Dennis has
done a lot of the parade preparation. He introduces me to Dan Pawelski,
the president of the JB/SA, and to Jay Dow, who will be "my driver." Jay
takes me to a 1965 Buick Electra 225 convertible that I will sit in and
wave to all the folks along the parade route.

At 11:15, the Clay Township fire trucks start the parade in front of
us. I sit on top of the back seat. I feel like I'm either a politician seeking
votes or Miss America as I wave to everyone standing in their yards.
Some of them recognize me. "Hey, Charlie!" Others have no clue who I

am or why I am waving to them. They look somewhat annoyed. Then there are those who have these sudden comments as I come by:

"Hey, it's the guy that does Sports!"

"Oh, look, Mike Collins!"

"It's that Charlie whats-his-name!"

"Hey, you're bigger in real life than on TV!"

"Hey, I know you! You're on the news."

"Show more hockey, Charlie!"

Many folks have cameras. What's funny is some will be poised to take a picture, then they'll realize it's me and lower their camera, preferring to save the shot for a smiling Little Leaguer. One bad thing about being Grand Marshall is you ride right behind the big firetrucks. That means a steady dose of black, billowing exhaust for three miles. After driving by what appears to be every house in north South Bend, we pull into Clay Park and the players rush to Weiler's Diamond. My last duty of the parade is to give a short talk, with the key word being "short." "Two years ago Tom Dennin talked for 30 minutes," one parent reminds me. "He went on forever. It was a fine talk, but my goodness I didn't think it would ever end."

"What I liked about Sheriff Joe Speybroeck's talk last year was that it was short," another parent adds.

Right then and there I mentally whittle my talk down from 10 minutes to three. So much for any long rambling tales of my Little League years.

During my talk, I "plead" with the parents to count to 10 before verbally shishkabobbing the umpires. I thank everyone and then hand the microphone back to Dennis Cooper so they can carry on with their program. Normally I stay for the completion of any program I'm invited to attend, but on this day I slip out the side gate because Sherrad and the kids are going to meet me at Randy and Janet Brooks' house in Elkhart for Sunday lunch and kids playtime. Jay Dow drives me back in the convertible to my car at Swanson. Jay's an assistant basketball coach at LaSalle, one of many men and women who mean so much to the young people of South Bend who don't get paid much for what they do.

As the convertible rumbles back through the neighborhood, we talk about who is going to be tough in the NIC basketball race in 1999.

"Washington has Kilgore back."

"Mishawaka has those two big kids."

"Clay will be tough, but you just don't replace a Lincoln Glass."

"I think our starting five at LaSalle can be as good as anyone. But it's the kids six through 10 that get you to Regional and Semi-State."

With the sun splashing down, I gaze at the passing houses. Being a sportscaster can drive a guy up the wall at times, but one things for sure: no day is ever the same in this line of work.

I would like to tell those of you who live in the Michiana area about a recent development at WSBT TV. As of November of 1998, Channel 22 has started a new 5:30 newscast. We've always done 5:00 to 5:30 and 6:00 to 6:30. Now there's a newscast in the middle. WHME-TV 46 will air it the part of the year when the "CBS Evening News" with Dan Rather airs on WSBT. Amanda Hart and I are anchoring the half hour, which will have a different look than most newscasts. Amanda will report news events of the day. Among the things I will concentrate on are the "Making A Difference" features and a regular feature on children. I also will do some fun "bits" from out in the field. So, if you have any feature ideas or fun story ideas (like your business doing something funny), please contact me at WSBT (219-232-6397).

Also, I'd like to tell you about "22 Listens" which is headed by Cindy Ward. If your community has a need or concern, please contact Cindy. She will assign several WSBT reporters and producers to come to one of your community or organization meetings to listen to the issues being discussed. Cindy will then coordinate coverage that brings attention to your particular community need. You can contact Cindy in the mid-afternoon at the number listed above.

Part Four
Charlie's Guide to the Biz and the Hidden Gems of Michiana Sports

Frank Advice on Getting into the TV News Sportscasting Business

Charlie,

My name is Chris Church and I am a freshman here at Ball State. I live in LaPorte and when I am home I watch Channel 22 for Sports. Here at Ball State I'm a Telecommunications major. I'm a sports reporter for our TV station, and co-host an hour long sports show for WCRD radio, which David Letterman started and still funds. I am now the play by play/color commentary announcer for baseball games and I am also a member of the National Broadcasting Society (NBS). This summer I will be working for WIPB here in Muncie, which is our PBS affiliate. I am a huge sports fanatic and would like to become a sports broadcaster someday. I was wondering if you could give me some advice or some direction in which I could reach my goal.

Sincerely,
Chris Church

I'm often asked by young folks how they should go about getting into sportscasting. There's no exact science, but what I'd like to do is share the path that took me into the Adventureland of Sportscasting and then give some tips that might be of help. Based on Chris' letter, he is already doing a lot of things that will help him become a professional sportscaster.

My Route

As a young kid, I was a sports nut. I was a huge fan of the Big Red Machine Cincinnati Reds in the 1970s. When my mother took a teaching job at Duke, I became an ACC basketball fanatic. I loved the New Orleans Saints because of my hero, quarterback Archie Manning. I followed golf because of Jack Nicklaus. I played just about every sport that was available. Add all this up and Sports was, by far, my passion. Like many people, I didn't even think that I could do something sports-related for a living. In high school, I developed a little (the key word is *little)* art ability so I decided to major in Graphic Arts in college. It didn't take long to realize I was average in that field so as a sophomore I changed my major to Education. The idea of being a coach and teacher was very appealing. When I heard there was a shortage of males in Elementary Education, I specified that as my new major (the fact that there were 25 girls and me in every class had NOTHING to do with it...). I was really enjoying the Education route at the University of Mississippi when early in my junior year I happened to be in Farley Hall, the Journalism Building. A piece of typing paper was taped to the main entrance with TRYOUTS in bold letters.

It caught my attention.

I moved closer and read that the student TV station was having tryouts for news anchor, sports anchor, and weather in a couple of days. Bang! It was like being tackled by Notre Dame's Kory Minor. For the first time, I saw an avenue to doing something professionally that had held my interest all my life. I went inside and met Bill Hampton who was in charge of the student TV News operation. Bill was from Muncie, Indiana. He was at Ole Miss (nickname for the University of Mississippi) to hopefully play baseball and get an education for a future in broadcasting. His intentions were to become a sportscaster, but at this particular time he was looking to get some experience as a news anchor. It would look good on his resume and help him become more balanced in broadcasting. Bill was very helpful to me and encouraged me to try out, despite the fact my major was in Education. I wrote down the tryout time and left the building excited with the possibilities.

I came back a couple of days later in my blue blazer and fat tie with an even fatter knot. I was so nervous I couldn't swallow. They had some prepared scripts for everyone to read into a studio camera. By the time my time came I was a basket case. Man, was I awful. I really wish I had saved that tape because it would get some bigtime laughs. For starters, I had more of a southern accent than all NASCAR drivers put together. I bobbed my head up and down and looked like a goober because of my big fat tie. But I got the sports anchor position. You want to know why? I was the only one that tried out for the position. Thank goodness a young Bobby Costas wasn't in the room.

My job was to do the sports Monday through Thursday on the evening newscast the student channel did for the local cable system. We were pretty rough around the edges, as you might imagine. From what I understand, the fraternity houses had the newscast on during their evening meal so they could get some good chuckles when a tape rolled wrong and we tried to react to it on live television. Still, it was tremendous experience for all of us and the product was pretty darn good when you consider we were so young. The guiding force was Jim Pratt, who did a wonderful job in running the TV News operation. Despite the fact that I was an Education major, he was tremendously helpful in guiding my passion for sportscasting. Often on Saturday mornings, I would drive to his house to get the key to the editing facilities. I still have his book, *A Primer for Broadcast Journalists*, at our house. On responsibility in broadcast journalism, Pratt writes, "A good news medium is fair, accurate, honest, responsible, independent and decent. Truth is its guiding principle." For all of you who think I'm a nut, Pratt's the guy who had the chance to stop me, but didn't!

Thanks to special help from student whiz kid Hampton, I was up and running in no time. After my Education classes in the morning, I hustled to the Journalism Building where I produced and edited my evening sportscast. With Ole Miss being in the prestigious Southeastern Conference, I had all sorts of premier coaches and athletes to interview. I remember Bill and I taking a news camera over to Starkville,

Mississippi, on a Wednesday night to cover Phi Slamma Jamma Houston at Mississippi State. I interviewed Akeem Olajuwon one-on-one courtside afterwards.

Looking to gain more experience, I started writing for the *Daily Mississippian*, which is the student newspaper. It was, and is, a very professional paper that didn't have the rough edges of the student TV newscast. The sports editor, Kate Magandy, showed me the ropes and I started cranking out articles like crazy.

Within a year, Hampton and I started a weekly 30-minute prime time TV show called "After the Buzzer." It was a talk show format where we would have guests in the studio as well as having taped features. By the time I was a senior, I had all sorts of experience. I often stayed at the student TV station until 2 AM editing features. Saturdays were spent covering Ole Miss football and basketball games. We traveled across the South with our cameras.

It didn't take me long to notice I was working much harder than many of the students who majored in Communications or Journalism. They were taking more classes in the subject than me, but many were just doing their required work after class and not much extra. I never did change my major to Communications, but did end up taking three of the most important Journalism classes as electives to add to all the experience I was gaining. The key word in all of this is EXPERIENCE. Next up was to get an internship at a TV station. WHBQ-TV in Memphis had an opening in Sports for the summer so I drove up and had an interview with Sports Director Paul Hartlage. Memphis is only about 80 miles away from Ole Miss. The interview went great and Paul tabbed me for the unpaid, but extremely valuable internship position. As soon as the spring semester was over, I got a small apartment in Memphis and started at WHBQ.

Now, this is key. Instead of sitting there in the office like a bump on the log everyday, I started looking for possible stories. I would get to the Sports office in the morning and by the time Paul arrived after lunch I had several "suggestions" for the department to cover. Paul was a great guy, a husky Minnesotian with a polished sportscasting style and a great voice. He never discouraged my enthusiasm. He told me when I had a dumb idea and when I had an idea that had possibilities. Instead of having me sit in the Sports office or fetch burgers, Paul put me to work in the field. Within a week I was going on stories with the Sports photographer. I was responsible for doing interviews that would be used on air. After the newscasts ended, I would take the raw tape and put together "practice" reports. Paul critiqued them and had a field day in kidding me about my southern accent. Within a month, Paul let me put together a short piece on the minor league Memphis Chicks' game for the 10 PM sportscast. It was short and sweet, but it was a great thrill and a stepping stone. From that point on I started doing two or three features a week that were aired. By no means was I good enough to anchor at that market size, but my feature reports were adequate.

I had one more semester at Ole Miss. As my summer internship ended, Paul and I arranged it with the WHBQ news director that I would freelance for the station in the fall. I would get paid $35 a story. My "beat" was covering Ole Miss football. I would cover their game on Saturday and then drive to WHBQ to do a story for the Saturday newscast. I would then stay until about 3 AM putting together two or three sidebar features that Paul would run that next week. I also spent the fall doing my student teaching at Pope Elementary, south of Batesville, Mississippi. It was a tremendous experience. I was basically in charge of the Physical Education programs for the kids for four months and had a blast. I could have been very satisfied being a coach at an upper elementary or middle school level where the emphasis was on development and encouragement of young people in sports, but I was building speed in broadcasting and had made the decision to pursue that career.

Upon graduating in December, I talked with Paul and WHBQ officials about a full-time position in Sports at their station. Paul did everything he could to convince management, but they did not want to add another position in Sports. I put together a video resume and looked in broadcast magazines for openings. I also had faculty in the Journalism Building who had numerous connections. One led me to an interview in Greenville, Mississippi, for the weekend sports anchor position. Sports Director Stan Sandroni took me to Popeye's Fried Chicken for the interview. He loved my resume tape and I think was going to offer me the position soon, but I saw an opening for sports director at WTOK-TV in Meridian, Mississippi. Sports director is the "boss" position in Sports. It's the guy who does the Sports Monday through Friday. I spruced up my video resume with several stories I had done in Memphis and drove down to Meridian. News Director John Johnson and I hit it off right from the start. My work in Memphis was the key in getting the position. Whereas other college applicants had shaky student TV work on their resume tapes, I had several reports that aired on a top 40 market station. I also had a segment showing me anchoring a sportscast from the WHBQ-TV studios.

Within a month of graduating from Ole Miss, I was a sports director at a small TV station, but a very respected station. WTOK-TV was, and is, extremely well run and it was an honor to be hired by them.

Where does the credit go for my move from a 20-year-old college junior with no experience to a 21-year-old hired as sports director without even having a degree in Communications? First, it goes to God for giving me the ability. Second, it goes to my mother, Dr. Anne H. Adams, who left me the money that paid for my college education. By not having to work jobs to pay for tuition, I was able to devote my time to gaining vital experience and education. I never had the gloom of financial loan payments hanging over my head. Third, it goes to the University of Mississippi, which is a tremendous place to gain experience as well as a broad education from the wide range of classes I took all over campus. Ole Miss is a major university without a huge enrollment. There's about 11,000 students there. I never felt like a number. I never had to go to a class in a massive auditorium where I was just a speck. Ole Miss is truly a special place. I wouldn't hesitate a bit to advise a high school student in the Midwest to seriously consider enrolling there. I would not have made it in the broadcast field without having gone to Ole Miss and without having met Dr. Jim Pratt and Bill Hampton (who is now #1 Sportscaster at WISH-TV in Indianapolis—he's known as Wil Hampton).

Now that you know a little bit about my path into TV News sportscasting, I'd like to share some advice that could be helpful if you want to go into the field. Your top priority should be to pray to God for Him to show you his will for your life. If sportscasting is what you think you would like to do, pray to God that He guide you in that direction. He very well might, or He might know of a better career for the gifts that He has blessed you with (and everyone has a gift from God).

As a high school student

• Write for the student newspaper. Study the work of the *South Bend Tribune* and *Elkhart Truth* sportswriters. Watch how they incorporate reporting the facts with unique writing styles. The *Tribune*'s Eric Hanson zings NFL draft expert Mel Kiper's hairstyle in writing an article on just one Notre Dame player being drafted. His story combines some wit, but its foundation is information on why Notre Dame had a down year. Start developing your style.

• Do the morning announcing for your high school. Do it in a way that is similar to a newscast. Find some friends who will report the news (announcements) of the day and then you take the microphone and announce what is going on in Sports at school. See if you can have a coach on hand for a live, short interview about a big game coming up soon.

• Many high schools nowadays have communications departments and/or equipment (something my high school did not have). Jump on that like white on rice.

• Contact WSBT about its' Explorers Program (233-3143). It is designed to give high school students a taste of what it's like to work at a TV station. If you don't live in the WSBT viewing area, contact your local TV stations about programs that might offer like this.

• Study the styles and writing techniques of all the sportscasters you have on your local stations, ESPN Sportscenter, CNN, Fox Sports News, and on and on. Never have there been so many sportscasters on the air.

Going into College

I am a big believer that you will have a better chance by going to a smaller college. My opinion is based on the fact I was able to do so many things at the University of Mississippi. Had I gone to Syracuse or Missouri, I would have faced much more competition because of their prestigious reputations in Journalism. WSBT has hired many graduates of Butler University in Indy (Lance McAlister and Matt Burridge are examples).

When researching possible colleges, you want to find a place where you will have virtually unlimited access to cameras, editing, and on-air positions. It will be UP TO YOU as to how fast you develop. Like most everything else, you will have to go ABOVE AND BEYOND the requirements of the degree. Going to college does not guarantee you will get a job as a TV News sportscaster. Hard work in college does not guarantee you will get a job. But if you combine the ability to report and anchor with a style that stands apart, you've got a good chance.

However, let me be frank about the TV news business. Sadly, in many ways it's a cosmetic business. You don't see many bald anchor men. Many stations look for anchors with hairlines like John F. Kennedy, Jr. It makes me so mad that I want to spit when I will approach a news director about a sports candidate and he or she will say, "his ears stick out" or "one eye seems to go a different direction." The emphasis on cosmetics is one reason I have never given total respect to the TV News field. I knew early on that I wasn't the best looking thing that ever came down the pike, but that has helped my career. I knew I would never be a "stud" who just has to sit out there and coast on looks. That made me realize I would always need a style and approach that set me apart. One thing you can control (usually) is your physical weight and fitness. I would never hire a sportscaster that was overweight. If a guy is going to cover sports, he'd better look like he can play them. Obviously, not like Tony Driver or A.J. Guyton, but you need to be fit. That's why, at age 36, I continue to lift weights and run 10 K's (5 K's before long. . . .).

Getting back to college, you will want to hook up with the college student newspaper and position yourself for an internship with a TV News station in your junior or senior year. I suggest you try to intern at a very small station where you can do all sorts of things and probably get on air. If you intern in Chicago, chances are your job will be to watch the sports video feeds that come down and go fetch hamburgers for the sports anchor.

The key is to build a solid resume tape by the end of your senior year. It should have three stories on it. One should be a report of a big game. Another should be on something like "is Creatine healthy or potentially dangerous to the many young athletes now taking it?" Then, have something fun on there like an evening at the local T-ball game. You should also have an anchor segment, though I suggest you start out as mainly a field reporter. Looking back, I wish I had been able to get out in the field more at the start of my career. Being sports director carries many administrative duties, and it required being at the desk a lot. WSBT's Mike Stack loves being able to come into the office, grab a camera, and head out into the field.

By the time you become a college senior, you will become aware of how to find openings to apply for in hopes of getting that first job. There are telephone numbers you can dial that update daily openings across the country. But realize that a whole bunch of folks will apply for the jobs. One time we announced an opening for the #3 position in Sports at WSBT and got about 250 applications from around the country. We had to stick the resume tapes in rooms all over the place. Cover letters had things like, "I will outwork anyone else. I will work for hardly anything." Not all stations get that many applications, but South Bend is one of the top Sports markets in America because of Notre Dame football and the aura of Indiana high school basketball. The bottom line is TO GET EXPERIENCE IN COLLEGE. Your G.P.A. is not as important as WHAT YOU CAN DO. I know that doesn't sound right, and that in most professions you'd better have a sparkling G.P.A., but I've seen many Communications students with 4.0 G.P.A.'s and plenty of book smarts who did dull reports and just didn't "have it."

The drawbacks of TV News

Let me make this clear. If you want to get married, start a family, and have a balanced family life soon after college, I suggest you DO NOT go into TV News. The hours are bizarre and often are the opposite of regular society. News directors often give lip service by asking about your family, but they could really care less. They'll work you to the bone. That's what I like about WSBT. Our news director Meg Sauer is married with 2 children. She's very understanding of family balance and priorities. She truly cares about how things are going at home.

Unless you're super stud anchor man or woman, it doesn't pay a lot. You have to work a lot of holidays. I've anchored sports several times on Christmas Day. I think it's pretty pathetic any station has a newscast on Christmas, but that's the way it is.

Unless your faith is strong, you can get off the right track. Looking back, when I started my first job as Sports Director in Meridian, Mississippi, I did not search for a church home in the city. Having been a Christian since I was a young teenager, that was a mistake that led to several years of getting away from Jesus in many areas of my life. That trend followed as I became sports director at KBAK-TV in Bakersfield, California, in 1985, after one year in Meridian. God is a patient God, though, and by the time I came to South Bend in 1988 I slowly began being pulled back into the arms of Jesus and repenting of sinful parts of my lifestyle. What I'm saying is that TV newsrooms are not exactly overflowing with Christians. Unless you have your spiritual armor on, you can make the mistake of spending too much time around people who don't know Christ. Next thing you know, you're doing some of the things they do. The Holy Spirit never let up on me, and the guilt connected led me out of that rut and into the mercy of God's forgiveness through repentance.

The positives of TV News

There are many. Don't let me scare you away by being frank about some of the things I've just discussed. A lot of that has to do with the fact that I had weak spiritual armor when I went into college and got away from reading the Bible and going to Church. I have enjoyed a very rewarding career, primarily because I have been able to serve others through my profession. I've been able to bring attention to worthy causes. I've been able to do stories on wonderful people. By airing the stories, others have been inspired by hearing that person.

The business can be unbelievably exciting. I've never tried a drug in my life. Why would I need to? There is no adrenaline rush like the daredevil atmosphere of putting together a Friday night sportscast. I've been on the sidelines of many thrilling contests. No day is the same. No hours are the same. Earlier, I talked about the odd hours. On the flip side, I'm in charge of my schedule. One day I might have a 12-hour day. The next day I might work seven hours. There are tons of opportunities to be creative. Editing is like putting together a painting. You have the elements of video and sound interviews. You get to mesh them together.

If you want to go into sportscasting "to be on TV," you're in for an eventual letdown. There's a lot of hard work behind the scenes. Seeing your face on camera is exciting for about 3 days. I've never been into that nonsense, though many are in the business for ego. Whatever. I will say this. Besides reporting the news, you can make a tremendous difference in your community if you go into sportscasting with the right intentions. You will have chances to do everything from being the Grand Marshall of a Little League parade to giving motivational speeches to being in a water dunk tank for charity to traveling to meeting famous people, and on and on.

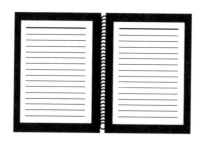

Charlie's Hidden Gems of Michiana Sports

Here are the activities, events, and places that I can't believe more people in the area don't go to see or participate in. I've been to them all as a reporter. I've also been to them all as a fan and with family. Check them out and I guarantee you'll be glad.

The Western Amateur: It gives you a feeling of what Augusta National is like during Masters week. The Point O'Woods course is breathtaking. It's rated as one of the Top 50 courses in America. The U.S. Amateur gets the national publicity, but the Western Am is a more challenging and grueling tournament than the U.S. Amateur. Western Amateur week is a great opportunity for couples to go up and just walk the course while taking in the outstanding golf. It's only about 45 minutes north of South Bend. Western Am week comes at the very end of July. Admission is just $5 and it goes towards scholarship money. If you need directions, call John "Mr. Western Amateur" Fineran at the *South Bend Tribune* Sports Department.

Notre Dame women's soccer: Sunday afternoon home games are wonderful family entertainment. My wife and I have taken the kids many times. During half-time there's a nearby field for youngsters to run around on. The games themselves are dynamite. Notre Dame's roster is filled with All-American and international caliber players.

Notre Dame women's basketball: (Not so hidden anymore as crowds are going up). This is wonderful family entertainment at a very affordable price. The basketball is pure and doesn't feature the rampant walking, traveling, and palming of the NBA.

Notre Dame women's softball: Ivy Field is tucked behind the Notre Dame football practice fields. In recent years, stands have been put up as well as a new scoreboard. The field is top-rate and the play is of Top-20 caliber. "A lot of people have the conception of softball that's it's slow pitch or rec ball," says Irish outfielder Jennifer Giampaola. "But this is serious. This is intense!" She's right. The pitcher fires the ball in there about 900 miles per hour. The defense is superb and the games are thrilling. "Just get the word out and let people know what is going on," says Notre Dame coach Liz Miller. "I think once they get out here and see the level of of competition we play, they're going to see it's a great thing to come and watch."

College Football Hall of Fame Grid Iron Legend Luncheons: This was started in 1997. Speakers such as Ohio State's Archie Griffin, Mississippi's Archie Manning, Notre Dame's Joe Theismann, and Purdue's Leroy Keyes have riveted the audience with their tales and motivational messages. Manning had me rolling in the floor with his stories of being QB on a bad Minnesota Vikings team. It was Archie's final year in the NFL. They were playing the awesome 1985 Bears team that would win the Super Bowl. Archie got sacked repeatedly by Richard Dent and company. Finally, Otis Wilson sacked him hard. As Archie was starting to get up, Otis looked at him and said, "Archie, if I were you, I'd just sit there and pretend you're injured." I highly recommend you take youngsters as the speakers often have strong positive messages. Michigan's Lloyd Carr gave a motivational talk that was very inspiring to the tables full of high school students from South Bend and middle school students from Michigan. The GridIron Luncheons are in the Press Box of the Hall of Fame or across the street in Century Center. They are in February, March, April, and May. There is talk of having some in the summer. Pick up the phone right now and call (219) 235-5707 to get tickets to the upcoming luncheons.

College Football Hall of Fame Stadium Theater: This is a powerful experience that will give your goosebumps. Former Mishawaka and Indiana University football player John Roggeman has seen it over

30 times and the hair on the back of his neck still stands up. CBS's Craig James was moved to tears after seeing it. Twenty movie screens wrap around the room, which gives you the feeling of Michigan Stadium as over 100,000 fans file in. The Stadium Theater experience takes you through Game Day in a powerful, pulsating way. Then, the decades of college football come swooping by you as greats such as Joe Paterno and Eddie Robinson talk about the passion of college football.

Flag Football game at FanFest: This is part of the annual Enshrinement Festival at the College Football Hall of Fame. FanFest is held on the GridIron Plaza right in front of the Hall. Inductees play a fun, full-speed-ahead game that brings a smile to the face of everyone watching in the bleachers. Grambling's Eddie Robinson coached the 1998 game. Notre Dame's Ken MacAfee, Nebraska's Dave Rimington and former Steeler Donnie Shell were among the players. The 1999 game is scheduled to feature Jim McMahon, Bo Jackson, and legendary coach Tom Osborne. You'd better get your tickets for that early. There's also a **Football Clinic** with the Hall-of-Famers at FanFest each year. If your youngster plays football at any level, don't miss it. Middle school coaches should make sure they get their team down there so there kids can get personal instruction from the greats.

The Michiana Sports Hall of Fame: It's in downtown Mishawaka on 109 Lincoln Way East (right next to the famous clock). It honors local sports stars. The first inductees were Lou Holtz, Ara Parseghian, Frank Leahy and Knute Rockne. The Hall is filled with colored portraits by local artists Tom and Gus Stangas. There's also a sports memorabilia shop connected to the Hall. The Michiana Sports Hall of Fame is open during the day Monday through Thursday. You can call 257-0039 for more information. Lawrence LaCluyse is the president, curator, and historian.

Team Notre Dame: This is a great way for your kids, grandkids, or any youngsters you know to get fired up about Notre Dame sports. It doesn't cost much to join. Members get free tickets to various Notre Dame games as well as chances to meet the athletes after certain games. There are contests and opportunities for the young folks to help others. Over $500 was raised by over 100 Team Notre Dame members in April 1998 for the Ara Parseghian Foundation. Kids got to run around Notre Dame Stadium in a mile-long race with Notre Dame athletes cheering them on. To get more info on Team Notre Dame call (219) 631-8393 or e-mail to teamnd@nd.edu

Bethel College Basketball: A lot of people know about their winning tradition and their national championships, but a lot of folks have not been to a game at the beautiful Wiekamp Athletic Center. Bethel's style of basketball will knock your socks off. The players dive all over the floor. The offense is high octane yet they play passionate defense. The games feature homegrown players and those competing are outstanding young men. You can walk up to the center on game day and purchase tickets. The student body support is special. Their enthusiasm and creativity makes me think of the Duke fans at Cameron Indoor Stadium.

Steve's Run: I love 10K's and this is one of my two favorites (along with Sunburst). Steve's Run is something you have GOT to take part in. There's the 10K and 5K for individuals and teams. There are fun and competitive walks for all ages. It starts in downtown Dowagiac and then you go through a golf course (with the golfers applauding you) and then through a cemetery into an enchanted forest with a wildlife refuge. The trails have hay bails and authentic Irish stone fences that you can either jump over (I always do) or go around. You then go through the campus of Southwestern Michigan College and back into the forest. Along the way music is played to fire you up and there are fun signs to draw laughter. One declares that "Luke Choate runs slower than a dry creek bed." After running the final phase on a quiet country road, you finish back in Dowagiac at a park that has a stream. Many runners jump in for a swim. There's a Summer Fun Fest amidst the beautiful Victorian Restoration of downtown Dowagiac. The incredible event is held in memory of Steven Briegel, a 1988 honors grad of SMC who died of cancer in 1990 after a very courageous and determined fight. "Steve's enthusiasm for life and his indefatigable spirit and strength will always serve as a source of inspiration and bravery for all those who knew him," says Ron Gunn, dean of Sports Education at SMC. Organizers sent almost $5,000 to the Mayo Clinic Cancer Research Fund and to the Briegel Scholarship Awards last year. Visit Steve's Run on the Web at www.michigan-runner.com/fireup/stevesrun for more info or call Ron Gunn at Southwestern Michigan College in Dowagiac (616)782-5113.

Macri's Deli Celebrity Party and Golf Outing: This happens annually in July. The party on a Sunday night is a great opportunity to talk with Notre Dame and sports legends. I have always wondered why more folks don't go out and watch the golf outing the next day. The admission is free and you can roam the golf course and get all sorts of autographs. There are many pro and college football players there along with NHL players and many other famous athletes and coaches. Call any Macri's Deli for more information.

Pro Basketball players at Bethel: Basketball fans, especially serious college basketball followers, will enjoy this annual event. It's run by former Elkhart Central star Jim Grandholm and former Wawasee High standout Mark Simpson. Their business, Accent Management International, guides the pro careers for many players. Every June dozens of very good players play at Bethel College for three days under the watchful eyes of scouts from the NBA, CBA, Europe, and other pro leagues. Past players include former Kentucky Wildcat Gimel Martinez, former Iowa State star Jeff Grayer, James Donaldson of the Dallas Mavericks, and Bethel's Rico Swanson. The games are open to the public and there's no admission charge. The 1999 three-day event is scheduled for June 3-5 at Bethel. Contact the Bethel Basketball Office for more details.

More Hidden Gems: Contact me at the WSBT Stations if you know of hidden sports gems in Michiana and I will write about them in the next book, which you have to buy or you will dissolve into wheat-like particles.

About the Author

Charlie Adams was born on July 9, 1962, in (William Faulkner country), Oxford, Mississippi. He graduated from the University of Mississippi with a degree in Elementary Education.

For 16 years, Charlie has been a TV News sportscaster in such markets as South Bend, Indiana; Bakersfield, California; New Orleans, Louisiana; and Meridian, Mississippi. During his broadcasting career, he has been awarded three Golden Microphones and the Associated Press/Broadcast Division Sportscaster of the Year.

Charlie has been sports director at WSBT-TV South Bend for eight years. He is married to the former Sherrad Bourn of Elkhart and has two children, Jack, age 6, and Abigail, age 3. The Adamses are members of Evangel Heights United Methodist Church.

TRAVELS WITH CHARLIE is his first book.